THE INTEGRATIVE
RESEARCH REVIEW

D1561433

Applied Social Research Methods Series
Volume 2

Applied Social Research Methods Series

Series Editor:
LEONARD BICKMAN, Peabody College, Vanderbilt University

Series Associate Editor:
DEBRA ROG, Joint Legislative Audit and
Review Commission, Commonwealth of Virginia

This series is designed to provide students and practicing profes-
sionals in the social sciences with relatively inexpensive soft-
cover textbooks describing the major methods used in applied
social research. Each text introduces the reader to the state of
the art of that particular method and follows step-by-step procedures in its explanation. Each author describes the theory
underlying the method to help the student understand the reasons for undertaking certain tasks. Current research is used to
support the author's approach. Examples of utilization in a variety of applied fields, as well as sample exercises, are included
in the books to aid in classroom use.

Volumes in this series:

1. **SURVEY RESEARCH METHODS,** Floyd J. Fowler, Jr.
2. **THE INTEGRATIVE RESEARCH REVIEW: A Systematic
   Approach,** Harris M. Cooper
3. **METHODS FOR POLICY RESEARCH,** Ann Majchrzak
4. **SECONDARY RESEARCH: Information Sources and Methods,**
   David W. Stewart
5. **CASE STUDY RESEARCH: Design and Methods,** Robert K. Yin
6. **META-ANALYTIC PROCEDURES FOR SOCIAL RESEARCH,**
   Robert Rosenthal

   Additional volumes currently in development

THE INTEGRATIVE RESEARCH REVIEW

A Systematic Approach

Harris M. Cooper

Applied Social Research Methods Series
Volume 2

SAGE PUBLICATIONS Beverly Hills London New Delhi

To Elizabeth

For information address:

SAGE Publications, Inc.
275 South Beverly Drive
Beverly Hills, California 90212

SAGE Publications India Pvt. Ltd.
C-236 Defence Colony
New Delhi 110 024, India

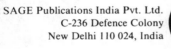

SAGE Publications Ltd
28 Banner Street
London EC1Y 8QE, England

Printed in the United States of America

Library of Congress Cataloging in Publication Data

Cooper, Harris M.
    The integrative research review.

    (Applied social research methods texts ; 2)
    Bibliography: p.
    1. Social sciences—Research. I. Title. II. Title:
Research review. III. Series.
H62.C5859   1984   300'.72   84-8227
ISBN 0-8039-2061-X
ISBN 0-8039-2062-8 (pbk.)

SECOND PRINTING, 1986

CONTENTS

PREFACE

Every research project in the social sciences should involve the inquirer searching out previous, related investigations. Without this step, an integrated, comprehensive picture of the world cannot be built. Researchers working in isolation repeat past mistakes and rarely achieve a sense of progress. Progress in social science comes from building on the efforts of those who have worked before.

Yet, the novice researcher has little guidance for how to conduct an integrative research review—how to find, evaluate, and synthesize previous research on the topic of interest. This book attempts to fill that void. It is intended for use by social science students with some background in basic research methods and statistics.

The approach to research reviewing espoused in this book represents a significant departure from how research reviews have been conducted in the past. Instead of the intuitive, subjective, narrative, style that has been the traditional approach to research reviewing, this book presents a systematic, objective alternative. This approach is rapidly gaining acceptance in many social science fields. The reader learns how to carry out problem formulations, literature searches, research evaluations, and research syntheses according to rules based on scientific principles. The intended result is a replicable review that can create consensus among scholars and focus debate in a constructive fashion. Most important, users of this approach should finish their reviews feeling knowledgeable about the research area and confident that their future primary research can make a contribution to the field.

Several institutions and individuals were instrumental in the preparation of this book. First, the National Institute of Education provided research support while the manuscript was prepared. The grant, entitled "A systematic examination of the literature review and knowledge synthesis activities," was overseen by Spencer Ward of the NIE's Dissemination in Practice Program.

Special thanks go to four former graduate students: Maureen Findley, Ken Ottenbacher, David Tom, and Julie Yu. Each performed a research review in their own area of interest under my supervision. Their efforts have been used throughout the book to illustrate abstract points. While they were becoming expert in their fields, I was learning about problems in reviewing that transcend topic areas as well as about many more unique reviewing difficulties.

Jeanmarie Fraser, a librarian at the University of Missouri's Elmer Ellis Library, spent many hours conducting computerized literature searches for me and my students. She also graciously gave me a crash course in library science.

The first draft of this volume was read and critiqued by twelve people: Len Bickman, Ruth Haber, Larry Hedges, Ken Ottenbacher, Jolene Pettis, Ronald Ribble, Debra Rog, Robert Rosenthal, David Schumann, David Tom, Tedra Walden, and Julie Yu. Each made comments that helped improve the final product.

Finally, the Center for Research in Social Behavior and especially its staff deserve my thanks. Patricia Shanks, Janice Meiburger, Terry Brown, and Diane Chappell transcribed, typed, and proofread the manuscript while tolerating a frenetic author. No simple task.

Columbia, Missouri   Harris Cooper

1

Introduction

This chapter presents a definition of the term "integrative research review," a justification for critical attention to research reviews, and a five stage research model for the reviewing process. The chapter also introduces four research reviews that serve as practical examples in the chapters that follow.

The pursuit of knowledge with the tools of science is a cooperative, interdependent process. The dozens or hundreds of hours spent conducting a scientific study ultimately contribute just one piece to an enormous puzzle. The value of any single study is derived as much from how it fits with and expands on previous work as from the study's intrinsic properties. Although it is true that some studies receive more attention than others, this is typically because the piece of the puzzle they solve (or the puzzle they introduce) is extremely important, not because they are solutions in and of themselves.

THE NEED FOR ATTENTION TO
RESEARCH REVIEWS

Given the cumulative nature of science, trustworthy accounts of past research form a necessary condition for orderly knowledge building. Yet, research methods textbooks in the social sciences show a remarkable lack of attention to how an inquirer finds, evaluates, and integrates past research. This inattention is especially troubling today because the social sciences have recently undergone a huge increase in the amount of research being conducted. To accommodate the expanding demand for communication, the number of outlets for theoretical and research reports has burgeoned.

The ability to gain access to social science information has also changed dramatically in recent years. In particular, retrieval of past work has been facilitated by the computerized literature search. The computer's ability to rapidly scan abstracts has improved interested scientists' access to evidence, if they know how to use the technology.

Finally, the need for trustworthy accounts of past research is also strengthened by growing specialization within the social sciences. Time constraints make it impossible for most social scientists to keep abreast of primary research except within a few topic areas of special interest to them. Garvey and Griffith (1971) wrote about this situation in psychology:

> The individual scientist is being overloaded with scientific information. Perhaps the alarm over an "information crisis" arose because sometime in the last information doubling period, the individual psychologist became overburdened and could no longer keep up with and assimilate all the information being produced that was related to his primary specialty. (p. 350)

GOALS AND PREMISES OF THE BOOK

The goal for this book is to compensate for the lack of attention given to the literature review in social science methods texts. It will apply the basic tenets of sound data gathering to a comprehensive synthesis of past research on a topic. The rules of rigorous, objective inquiry are the same whether the inquirer is conducting a primary study or a research review. The two types of inquiry, however, require techniques specific to their purpose and the techniques for integrative research reviewing have largely been ignored in the past.

The underlying premise of this treatment is that *locating and integrating separate research projects involves inferences as central to the validity of knowledge as the inferences involved in primary data interpretation*. Due to the amount and diverse locations of social science information, the comprehensiveness and validity of review conclusions can no longer be taken for granted. A scientist performing a research review makes numerous decisions that affect the outcome of the review and each choice may create threats to the outcome's trustworthiness. Therefore, if social science knowledge transmitted through research reviews is to be objective and believable, *research reviewers must be required to use the same rigorous methodology that is required of primary researchers*.

While substantial attention has been paid to validity issues in primary research (Campbell & Stanley, 1963; Campbell, 1969; Bracht & Glass, 1968; Cook & Campbell, 1979), the social sciences lack a conceptualization of the research review process that provides systematic guidelines for evaluating the validity of review outcomes. This book is an attempt to provide such an organizing scheme.

DEFINITIONS OF LITERATURE REVIEWS

Literature reviews typically appear as introductions to reports of new primary data or as more detailed independent works (e.g., Maccoby & Jacklin, 1974; Harper, Weins, & Matarazzo, 1978). The scope of a literature review that introduces new data is typically quite narrow. Research cited as an introduction to other primary research will be restricted to those studies pertinent to the specific issue addressed by the new data.

When a literature review appears independent of new data, it can serve decidedly broader purposes. Three types of reviews with different purposes can be identified. The first type of literature review is the *integrative research review*. Integrative reviews summarize past research by drawing overall conclusions from many separate studies that are believed to address related or identical hypotheses. The integrative reviewer hopes to present the state of knowledge concerning the relation(s) of interest and to highlight important issues that research has left unresolved. From the readers's viewpoint, an integrative research review is intended to "replace those earlier papers that have been lost from sight behind the research front" (Price, 1965, p. 513), and to direct future research so that it yields a maximum amount of new information.

The second kind of literature review is a *theoretical review*. Here, the reviewer hopes to present the theories offered to explain a particular phenomenon and to compare them with regard to their breadth, internal consistency, and the nature of their predictions. Theoretical reviews will typically contain descriptions of critical experiments already conducted or suggested, assessments of which theory is most powerful and consistent with known relations, and sometimes reformulations or integrations of abstract notions from different theories.

A third kind of review is a *methodological review*. Its intent is to examine the research methods and operational definitions that have been applied to a problem area. Methodological reviews are often critical of existing research, arguing that artifacts have produced results, that measurement has been untrustworthy, and/or that conditions limit the conclusions that can be drawn.

Often a comprehensive review will address two or all of these sets of issues. Integrative research reviews are probably most common, however, and theoretical or methodological reviews will typically contain some integrative review components. It is also not unusual for integrative reviews to address multiple, related hypotheses. For instance, a review might examine the relation between several different independent variables and a single dependent variable, or it might try to summarize research related to a series of temporally linked hypotheses.

The major emphasis of this book will be the integrative research review. Not only is this review most common, but it also contains all the decision points present in other reviews—and some unique points as well.

THE STAGES OF RESEARCH REVIEW

Most textbooks on research methodology suggest that scientific inquiry involves a temporally sequenced set of activities (see Kerlinger, 1973; Rosenthal & Rosnow, 1975). Although methodologists differ in the subtlety of their definitions for research stages, the most important distinctions in stages can be identified with a gratifying degree of consensus. Methodologists also uniformly agree that the sequencing of stages is not fixed; practicing researchers often skip over one or more stages and sometimes move backward as well as forward (Selltiz, Wrightsman, & Cook, 1976).

In this book, the process of integrative research reviewing will be conceptualized as containing five stages or phases: (1) problem formulation; (2) data collection; (3) evaluation of data points; (4) analysis and interpretation; and (5) presentation of results. Each stage of the review serves a function similar to the one it serves in primary data research. For example, in both primary research and research review the problem formulation stage involves the definition of variables, and the analysis and interpretation stage involves making a choice about what results are significant. Reviewers, like primary data collectors, can make different choices about how to carry out their inquires. Differences in review methodologies will create variation in review conclusions. Most importantly, each methodological choice at each stage of a review may undermine the trustworthiness of the review's conclusion, or in more scientific terms, create a threat to the review's validity. (A more formal definition of validity appears in Chapter 4.)

The functions, sources of variance, and potential threats to validity associated with each stage of the review process are summarized in Figure 1.1. In the chapters that follow, each stage of the research review will be examined in greater detail.

Problem formulation stage. The first stage in the research process is the problem formulation stage. During problem formulation, the variables involved in the inquiry are given both abstract and concrete definitions. At this stage the researcher asks: "What operations are relevant to the concepts that concern the review?" More broadly, the researcher must decide what distinguishes relevant from irrelevant material.

In Chapter 2, the decision points encountered by a reviewer during the problem formulation stage are discussed. Included in this discussion will be answers to the following questions: (a) What affects a reviewer's decisions about the conceptual relevance of particular studies? (b) How should a reviewer handle hypotheses that involve the interaction of two or more independent variables? and (c) What role should past reviews play in formulating a problem? Chapter 2 will also present some concrete recommendations

Stage Characteristics

Stage of Research

Stage Characteristics	Problem Formulation	Data Collection	Data Evaluation	Analysis and Interpretation	Public Presentation
Research Question Asked	What evidence should be included in the review?	What procedures should be used to find relevant evidence?	What retrieved evidence should be included in the review?	What procedures should be used to make inferences about the literature as a whole?	What information should be included in the review report?
Primary Function in Review	Constructing definitions that distinguish relevant from irrelevant studies.	Determining which sources of potentially relevant studies to examine.	Applying criteria to separate "valid" from "invalid" studies.	Synthesizing valid retrieved studies.	Applying editorial criteria to separate important from unimportant information.
Procedural Differences That Create Variation in Review Conclusions	1. Differences in included operational definitions. 2. Differences in operational detail.	Differences in the research contained in sources of information.	1. Differences in quality criteria. 2. Differences in the influence of nonquality criteria.	Differences in rules of inference.	Differences in guidelines for editorial judgment.
Sources of Potential Invalidity in Review Conclusions	1. Narrow concepts might make review conclusions less definitive and robust. 2. Superficial operational detail might obscure interacting variables.	1. Accessed studies might be qualitatively different from the target population of studies. 2. People sampled in accessible studies might be different from target population of people.	1. Nonquality factors might cause improper weighting of study information. 2. Omissions in study reports might make conclusions unreliable.	1. Rules for distinguishing patterns from noise might be inappropriate. 2. Review-based evidence might be used to infer causality.	1. Omission of review procedures might make conclusions irreproducible. 2. Omission of review findings and study procedures might make conclusions obsolete.

Figure 1.1: The Integrative Review Conceptualized as a Research Project

SOURCE: Cooper, H., "Scientific guidelines for conducting integrative research reviews." *Review of Educational Research*, 1982, 52, 291-302. Copyright 1982, American Educational Research Association, Washington, D.C. Reprinted by permission.

about what information a reviewer should collect from empirical studies that have been judged relevant to a problem area.

Data collection stage. The data collection stage of research involves making a choice about the population of elements that will be the focus of the study. Identifying populations for research reviews is complicated by the fact that the reviewer wants to make inferences about two targets. First, the reviewer wants the cumulative result of the review to be based on all previous research on the problem. Second, the reviewer hopes that the included studies will allow generalizations to the population of individuals (or other units) that are the focus of the topic area.

Chapter 3 presents a detailed discussion of methods for locating studies. The discussion includes a listing of the sources of studies available to social scientists, how to use the most important sources, and what biases may be present in the information contained in each source.

Data evaluation stage. After data are collected, the inquirer makes critical judgments about the quality of individual data points. Each data point is examined in light of surrounding evidence to determine whether it is contaminated by factors irrelevant to the problem under consideration.

Chapter 4 discusses how evaluations of research quality can be carried out and makes some suggestions concerning the assessment of interjudge reliability and where biases in judgments come from. Also, Chapter 4 contains some recommendations concerning unavailable research reports and reports that are incomplete.

Analysis and interpretation stage. During analysis and interpretation, the separate data points collected by the inquirer are synthesized into a unified statement about the research problem. Interpretation demands that the inquirer distinguish systematic data patterns from "noise" or chance fluctuation.

Chapter 5 contains an explanation of some methods for combining the results of separate studies and for estimating the size or magnitude of a relation. Some techniques for analyzing the difference in relation size found in different studies are also examined.

Public presentation stage. Creating a public document that describes the review is the task that completes a research endeavor. In Chapter 6, some concrete guidelines will be offered on how to report integrative research reviews.

FOUR ILLUSTRATIONS OF
RIGOROUS RESEARCH REVIEW

The best way to demonstrate both the feasibility and benefits of rigorous research reviewing is through example. For this reason, four research reviews conducted by social science graduate students under this author's tutelage have been chosen to illustrate the practical aspects of conducting integrative research reviews using the guidelines specified herein. The topics of the four reviews represent a broad spectrum of social science research, encompass qualitatively different kinds of research, and involve diverse conceptual and operational variables. Even though the topics are diverse, they are also general enough that readers in any discipline should find all four topics instructive and easy to follow without a large amount of background in the separate research areas. However, a brief introduction to each topic will be helpful.

Locus of control and academic achievement (Findley & Cooper, 1983). One topic that has intrigued both psychologists and educators is the relation between locus of control beliefs and achievement in school. Locus of control refers to people's feelings about whether they control the events in their life. Some people, labeled internals, feel more responsible for the things that happen to them. Other people, labeled externals, feel that their outcomes in life are determined more by forces beyond their control, for example, fate or other people.

The prediction that a stronger belief in internal locus of control will be associated with higher academic achievement is both logical and consistent with social theory (Rotter, 1954). People who feel more able to control the outcome of events should exert more effort to do so. Also, internals should experience more pride when they succeed and more shame when they fail. Thus the rewards and punishments experienced in school by internals should be stronger and, therefore, more motivating than those experienced by externals.

In discussing the goals of the review, then, Findley and Cooper, (1983) wrote:

> This review has two primary goals: (a) to obtain an estimate of the strength, as well as direction, of the relation between locus of control and academic achievement, and (b) to examine those variations in people, settings, and instruments that appear to influence the relation's strength (p. 420).

Social class and ethnic group differences in achievement motivation (Cooper & Tom, 1984). McClelland and his colleagues (1953) define achievement motivation as "affect in connection with evaluation" (p. 79). They state that "whether the performance be grooming, playing football, landing a job or herding sheep, it can give evidence of an achievement motive if there is affect or involvement connected with evaluation of it" (p. 80). Higher achievement motivation means greater desire to be successful and greater affect following success and failure.

Differences in people's levels of achievement motivation have been explained by differences in child-rearing practices. In particular, the amount of independence training, or the fostering of behaviors that encourage self-reliance and autonomy, have been suggested as a source of differences in the need to achieve. In turn, child-rearing practices are correlated with the economic conditions and cultural prescriptions that surround the family.

Do social classes and ethnic groups differ in need for achievement? This question has been asked and tested repeatedly since the concept of achievement motivation was first formulated. David Tom and this author (1984) undertook the task of collecting and summarizing the research that related people's need for achievement to their economic or ethnic backgrounds.

Drug treatment of hyperactive children (Ottenbacher & Cooper, 1983). Hyperactivity, a disorder involving a deficit in attention, has been estimated to afflict between 4% and 20% of school-aged children. Due to its frequency, both educators and physicians have vigorously pursued effective treatments for hyperactivity. The proposed treatments range from dietary restrictions and supplements to behavior modification training. By far the most prevalent treatment of hyperactivity, however, is pharmacological management and almost all children identified as hyperactive receive some form of drug therapy in the course of their treatment.

Although drug treatment of hyperactivity is so frequently prescribed, there is still substantial controversy over the advisability of its use. In addition there has been some question about the relative effectiveness of different types of drugs (stimulants and nonstimulants) and about any drug's ability to affect behaviors beyond simple motor or perceptual performance (i.e., social adjustment and educational performance).

The research review undertaken by Ken Ottenbacher and this author was intended to address three of these outstanding issues. Specifically, the primary questions the review was meant to answer were these: (a) What is the impact of the placebo effect on drug treatments of hyperactivity? (b) Do different drugs differ in their effect on hyperactivity? and (c) Is the effect of drug treatment generalizable to the social and educational behavior of hyperactive children?

Response rates to questionnaires (Yu & Cooper, 1983). One problem that plagues all the social sciences and marketing research in particular is nonresponse to survey questionnaires. When people are chosen for inclusion in a study but refuse or are unable to take part in it, the researcher must confront the possibility that the remaining sample is no longer representative of the target population.

Numerous techniques have been employed to maximize questionnaire response rates (Kanuk & Berensen, 1975). These include preliminary notification that a questionnaire is coming, cover letters with different types of appeals, personalization of the request, inclusion of return envelopes and postage, monetary and nonmonetary incentives, and follow-up contacts, to name a few.

Past reviews of the effectiveness of these techniques have concluded that there was no strong support for the value of any technique other than the use of monetary incentives and follow-up contacts (Kanuk & Berensen, 1975). These reviews, however, were narrative syntheses of research. Julie Yu and this author attempted to go beyond past efforts by conducting a quantitative synthesis of the research literature. It was stated that because "response rates (or responses as a percent of the size of the contacted samples) are a universal measure of the effectiveness of a technique, the results [i.e., raw data] of studies which used the same technique [can be directly] arithmetically combined" (pp. 36-37). Conducting such an analysis was the purpose of this review.

EXERCISE

The best exercise to carry out while reading this book is to conduct an integrative research review in an area of interest to you. The review should attempt to apply the guidelines explicated in the chapters that follow. If such an exercise is not possible, try to conduct the more discrete exercises that appear at the end of each chapter. Often, these exercises can be further simplified by dividing the work among members of your class.

2

The Problem Formulation Stage

This chapter describes the process of formulating a hypothesis for guiding an integrative research review. Topics include the treatment of concepts and operations, the distinction between study-generated review-generated evidence, the treatment of main effects and interactions, the role of previous reviews in new reviewing efforts, the development of coding sheets for primary research reports, and the threats to validity during problem formulation.

"No matter what problem you want to work on and no matter what method you will eventually use, your empirical work *must* begin with a careful consideration of the research problem" (Simon, 1978, p. 98). In its most basic form, the research problem includes the definition of variables and the rationale for relating the variables to one another. The rationale can be that a theory predicts a particular association between variables (as in confirmatory research) or that some other practical or intuitive consideration suggests that *any* discovered relation might be important (as in exploratory research). Either problem rationale can be used for undertaking primary research or a research review.

The choice of a relation to study in primary research is influenced by the interests of researchers and the social conditions that surround them (Selltiz, et al., 1976). This holds true for the choice of a topic by prospective research reviewers as well, with an important restriction. Primary researchers are limited only by their imaginations but research reviewers must study topics that already appear in the literature. In fact, a topic is probably not suitable for review unless it has appeared in the literature and has created appreciable interest within a discipline, either because the problem is of broad conceptual caliber or because it is surrounded by intense research activity.

The fact that reviews are tied to a finite universe of problems does not mean the activity of research synthesis is any less creative than primary research. Instead, the creativity in research review enters when reviewers are asked to make sense of many related but not identical theories or studies. More often than not, the cumulative results of studies are many times more complex than envisioned by the separate researchers who conducted them. The reviewer's instinct for uncovering variables that influence a relation and ability to generate divergent schemes are important ingredients in the research synthesis process.

DEFINITION OF VARIABLES
IN SCIENTIFIC INQUIRY

Similarities Between Primary Research and Research Review

The variables involved in a scientific inquiry must be defined in two ways. First, the variables must be given conceptual definitions. These describe qualities of the variable that are independent of time and space but which can be used to distinguish events that are and are not relevant to the concept (Carlsmith, Ellsworth, & Aronson, 1976). For instance, a conceptual definition of "aggression" might be "a physical attack by one person on another." Conceptual definitions can differ in abstractness, or in the number of events to which they refer. Thus, if "aggression" is defined as "a tendency toward hostile action," the concept is more abstract than the first definition. The second definition would consider verbal taunts and facial expressions "aggression," as well as acts by nonhuman species. Both primary researchers and research reviewers must choose a conceptual definition and a degree of abstractness for their problem variables. Both must decide how likely it is that an event represents an instance of the variable of interest.

In order to relate concepts to concrete events, a variable must also be operationally defined. An operational definition is a set of instructions describing the observable events that allow one to determine if a concept is present in a particular situation (Reynolds, 1971). An operational definition of aggression might include "loud verbal exchanges." Again, both primary researchers and research reviewers must specify the operations included in their variable definitions.

Differences Between Primary Research and Research Review

Some differences between the two types of inquiry can also be found in variable definition. Primary researchers have little choice but to define their concepts operationally before the inquiry begins. Primary data collection cannot start until variables have been given some circumscribed empirical reality. Reviewers, on the other hand, need not be quite so theoretically rigorous. The literature search can begin with only a conceptual definition. The research reviewer has the comparative luxury of being able to evaluate the conceptual relevance of different operations as they appear in the literature or simultaneously with data collection. Of course, some a priori specification of operations is desirable and most reviewers do begin with empirical realizations in mind. It is not unusual, however, for a reviewer to stumble upon operations that were not initially considered but that, upon inspection, the reviewer decides are relevant to the construct. In sum, a primary researcher usually knows exactly what events constitute the domain to be sampled before data collection begins but a reviewer may discover unanticipated samplings along the way.

A more significant distinction between the types of inquiry is that primary research typically involves only one, and sometimes two, operational definitions of the same construct. In contrast, research reviews usually involve many empirical realizations. Although no two participants are treated exactly alike in any single study, this variation will ordinarily be small compared to that introduced by the differences in laboratories, treatments, measurements, sampled population, and analysis techniques used in separate studies (see Pillemer & Light, 1980). The multiple operations contained in research reviews introduce a set of unique problems that need to be examined carefully.

MULTIPLE OPERATIONS
IN RESEARCH REVIEW

The "fit" between concepts and operations. Research reviewers undertaking the formulation of a problem must be aware of two potential incongruities that may arise because of the variety of operations in the literature. First, the reviewer anticipating multiple operations may begin a literature search with a broad problem definition but find that the operations used in previous relevant research have been quite narrow. For instance, the illustrative review of the relation between locus of control and achievement might have begun with a broad definition of achievement, including the academic, social, political, and economical spheres of behavior. If this were the case, the result would have been disappointing, since the vast majority of past research dealt only with achievement in academic matters. When such a circumstance arises, the reviewer must narrow the conceptual underpinnings of the review to be more congruent with operations. Otherwise, the conclusions of the review will appear more general than the data warrant.

The opposite problem, using narrow concepts defined by multiple, broad measures, can also confront a reviewer. This would have occurred if the locus of control and achievement review had initially sought only academic measures of achievement but the literature search revealed many other types of achievement behavior. The reviewer then faces the choice of either broadening the concept or excluding many studies.

It is extremely important that a reviewer take care to reevaluate the correspondence between the level of abstractness of a concept definition and the representativeness of the operations that primary researchers have used to define it. While such redefinition of the problem as an inquiry proceeds is frowned upon in primary research, it appears that some flexibility may be necessary, if not beneficial, in research review.

Multiple operationism and concept-to-operation correspondence. Webb, Campbell, Schwartz, Sechrest, and Grove (1981) presented strong arguments for the value of multiple operationism. They define multiple operationism as the use of many measures that supposedly share a theoretical concept "but have different patterns of irrelevant components" (p. 35). Multiple operationism has positive consequences because

> once a proposition has been confirmed by two or more independent measurement processes, the uncertainty of its interpretation is greatly reduced. . . . If a proposition can survive the onslaught of a series of imperfect measures, with all their irrelevant error, confidence should be placed in it. Of course, this confidence is increased by minimizing error in each instrument and by a reasonable belief in the different and divergent effects of the sources of error. (p. 35)

While Webb and colleagues (1981) hold out the potential for strengthened inferences due to multiple operations, their qualification must also be underscored. Multiple operationism can enhance concept-to-operation correspondence if all or most of the measures encompassed in the research review are of at least satisfactory validity. This reasoning is akin to the reasoning applied in classical measurement theory to the single items on a personality questionnaire. Small correlations between individual items (in this case operations) and a "true" score can add up to a reliable indicator *if* a sufficient number of minimally valid items (operations) are present. However, if the majority of operations bear no correspondence to the underlying concept or the operations share a different concept to a greater degree than they share the intended one, the conclusion of the review will be invalid regardless of how many items or operations are involved, also analogous to personality measurement theory.

The research reviewer also must examine research designs for threats to the correspondence of operations and concepts. If the research designs uncovered by a literature search all contain the same invalidating procedures, then the correspondence between operations and concepts is threatened. The illustrative review of research concerning ethnicity and the need for achievement provides a good example. A study by Lefkowitz and Fraser (1980) compared whites and blacks using the Thematic Apperception Test, or TAT. The TAT may be a valid measure of need for achievement and the researchers may also have been able to classify perfectly whites and blacks with regard to their ethnic heritage. However, the Lefkowitz and Fraser (1980) study did not control for the social class of participants. That is, whites in their sample were found to be of higher social class than blacks. Therefore, although their measure of ethnicity was perfectly valid, it also allowed for the natural confusion of social class differences with ethnic differences. If all of the studies uncovered by the literature search contained this same confounding, then the fact that the ethnicity indicators were perfectly reliable and valid could not be used to rebuff the rival hypothesis that social class accounted for any ethnic differences. Luckily, the literature search also uncovered several studies that did control for social class and these produced results similar to studies which did not control social class.

Uncontrolled participant characteristics are not the only research design problem that can be reduced by the multiple operations sometimes contained in research reviews. For instance, in the review of drug treatments of childhood hyperactivity, some studies were found that kept only physicians (administers of the treatment) blind to whether they were giving a placebo or drug while other studies kept only recorders of the dependent variables blind. If results across both types of studies are similar, the possibility that expectancy effects explain the results is less plausible when the accumulated findings are examined.

In sum then, the existence of multiple operations in research literatures presents the potential benefit of stronger inferences through "triangulation" of evidence. However, multiple operations do not ensure concept-to-operation correspondence if all or most of the measures lack minimal correspondence to the concept or if research designs all share a similar confounding of unintended influences with intended ones.

Substituting new concepts for old ones. Perhaps the most challenging circumstance in the social sciences occurs when a new concept is introduced to explain old findings. For example, in social psychology the notion of cognitive dissonance has been employed frequently to explain why an individual paid $1 to voice a counterattitudinal argument subsequently experiences greater attitude change than another person paid $25 to perform the same activity (Festinger & Carlsmith, 1959). Dissonance theory suggests that because the amount of money is not sufficient to justify the espousal of the counterattitudinal argument, the person feels discomfort that can be reduced only through a shift in attitude. However, Bem (1967) recast the results of these dissonance experiments by invoking a self-perception theory. Briefly, he speculated that participants who observe themselves espousing counterattitudinal arguments infer their opinions the same way an observer would. Participants who see themselves making an argument for $1 assume that because they are performing the behavior with little justification they must feel positive toward the attitude in question.

No matter how many replications of the $1/$25 experiment are uncovered, a research reviewer could not use the results to evaluate the correctness of the two theories. The research reviewer must take care to differentiate concepts and theories that predict similar and different results for the same set of operations. If predictions are different, the accumulated evidence can be used to evaluate the correctness of one theory or another, or the different circumstances in which each theory is correct. If, however, the theories make identical predictions, no comparative judgment based on research outcomes is possible.

The use of operations not originally related to the concept. Literature searches often uncover research that has been cast in a conceptual framework different from the reviewer's but which includes measures or manipulations relevant to the concepts the reviewer had in mind. For instance, there are several concepts similar to "locus of control" that appear in research. When relevant operations associated with different abstract constructs are identified, they most certainly should be considered for inclusion in the review. In fact, different concepts and theories behind similar operations can often be used to demonstrate the robustness of results. There is probably no better way to ensure that operations contain different patterns of irrelevant components than to have different researchers with different theoretical backgrounds perform related experiments.

The effects of multiple operations on review outcomes. Operational multiplicity does more than introduce potentially stronger inferences to conceptual variables. It is also the most important source of variance in the conclusions of different reviews meant to address the same topic. Operational multiplicity can affect review outcomes in two ways:

1. *Variance in operational definitions.* The operational definitions used in two research reviews on the same topic can vary. As noted earlier, two reviewers using an identical label for an abstract concept can employ very different operational definitions or levels of abstraction. Each definition may contain some operations excluded by the other, or one reviewer's definition may completely contain the other.

2. *Variance in operational detail.* Operational multiplicity also affects review outcomes by allowing reviewers to vary in their attention to methodological distinctions in the literature. This effect is attributable to differences in the way study operations are treated *after* the literature has been searched. Research reviewers, as Cook and Leviton (1981) note, "become detectives who use obtained data patterns as clues for generating potentially explanatory concepts that specify the conditions under which a positive, null, or negative relationship holds between two variables" (p. 462). Reviewers differ in how much detective work they undertake. Some reviewers may pay careful attention to study operations. They may decide to identify meticulously the operational and sample distinctions among retrieved studies. Other reviewers may feel that method- or participant-dependent relations are unlikely or they may simply use less care.

The illustrative reviews. Two of the four illustrative research reviews provide contrasting examples with regard to the broadness of their definitions, their fit between concepts and operations, and the impact of multiple operations on their findings.

The search for locus of control and academic achievement studies uncovered and included 22 different measures of locus of control. Clearly, multiple operations have been used in this area. Thus it is fairly certain that other personality variables confounded with locus of control on individual tests had little effect on the review's conclusions because multiple operations were used. However, while the broad notion of locus of control may appear to be covered by the 22 different measures, nearly all of the measures were of a paper-and-pencil variety. Therefore, we must still entertain the possibility that confounds associated with paper-and-pencil tests in general (like the social desirability of answers and evaluation apprehension) may still be confounded in this review's result.

In the locus of control review, 36 different measures of academic achievement were retrieved. These 36 measures could be categorized as (a) standardized achievement tests, (b) measures of intelligence, and (c) classroom related measures, including examination scores, grades, and teacher ratings. Given that the standardized measures included tests of both quantitative and verbal skills, we can be fairly confident that the broad concept "academic achievement" was covered by the varying operationalizations, though some might argue that the inclusion of intelligence measures made the concept too broad.

The review involving the effects of research design on questionnaire response rates presented the least difficulty with regard to problem formulation. The dependent variable, response rates to questionnaires, was identical across all studies. This is an instance in which very narrow conceptual and operational definitions are perfectly commensurate with the review's objectives. Similarly, the research designs covered by the review were all operationally defined. Thus, while about two dozen different research designs were examined (e.g., cover letters, monetary incentives), there was no need to propose an overarching conceptual variable to encompass them all (other than "research design," of course).

JUDGING THE CONCEPTUAL
RELEVANCE OF STUDIES

In presenting the operations included in two illustrative reviews and relating these to the reviewers' abstract notions, a more fundamental question was sidestepped: How were studies judged to be conceptually relevant in the first place? The rules the reviewer uses to distinguish relevant from irrelevant studies determine the degree of "fit" between concepts and operations.

Information scientists have closely scrutinized the question of what makes a study relevant to a research problem (Saracevic, 1970). Regrettably, the degree of concept abstractness that a reviewer employs has not been examined as an influence on the relevance judgement. It has been shown, however, that judgements about the relevance of studies to a literature search are related to a reviewer's openmindedness and expertise in the area (Davidson, 1977), the way the research is documented in the retrieval system (Resnick, 1961), and even the amount of time the reviewer has for making relevance decisions (Cuadra & Katter, 1967). Thus, while the conceptual definition and level of abstractness that a reviewer chooses for a problem are certainly two influences on the studies deemed relevant, a multitude of other factors also affect this screening of information.

The only general recommendation that can be made with regard to conceptual relevance is that the reviewer should begin the literature search with the broadest conceptual definition in mind. In determining the acceptability of operations for inclusion within the broad concept, the reviewer again should remain as open-minded as possible. At later stages in the review, notably during data evaluation, it is possible for a reviewer to exclude particular operations due to their lack of relevance or impurity. In the problem formulation and search stages, however, the reviewer should err on the overly inclusive side, just as a primary researcher collects some data that might not be used in analysis. It is most distressing to find out *after* studies have been retrieved and catalogued that available pieces of the puzzle were passed over and that the search must be reconstituted.

The broader search also allows the reviewer to undertake a review with greater operational detail. The benefits of broad conceptualization are underscored many times in the chapters that follow.

The illustrative reviews. As an example of conceptual relevance, the review of social class and ethnic differences in need for achievement faced the problem of whether to exclude particular ethnic groups or studies conducted in different countries. Most of the studies found in the literature search were conducted in the United States, but quite a few one-shot, international comparisons were made. Ultimately, all ethnic group comparisons were included in the review, regardless of their national or international flavor. On the other hand, a single study that employed a behavioral measure of need for achievement (i.e., persistence on a task) was excluded from the review, which otherwise included strictly verbal indicators of achievement striving. The single occurrence of a behavioral measure would have little affect on the outcomes of the review, but it might have been misleading to include it. Certainly its inclusion would not justify a claim that the overall results were applicable to behavioral indicators as well as verbal ones.

The drug treatments and response rate reviews presented few cases in which studies were difficult to classify as relevant or irrelevant, because the narrow objectives of these reviews meant there was little variation in method from one relevant study to another.

RELATIONS BETWEEN DIFFERENT CONCEPTS IN RESEARCH REVIEWS

The problems that motivate most research reviews initially involve relations between two variables. There is a simple explanation for this: main effects have typically been tested more often than any given interaction involving the same three variables. All four of the research reviews serving as illustrations took a bivariate relation as their initial focus. Each review, however, also examined potential influences on the main effect relation. The review of locus of control and achievement research, for instance, first looked at whether a relation between the two variables existed. Having answered this question affirmatively, it then went on to examine potential interacting variables. These moderators included the gender, educational level, and racial background of individuals.

While some specific interactional hypotheses in the social sciences may have generated enough interest to require independent research review, for the vast majority of topics the initial problem formulation will involve a main effect question. Again, however, the initial undertaking of the review to establish the existence of a main effect should in no way diminish the reviewer's attention to the interactive or moderating influences that may be discovered. If main effect relations are found to be moderated by third variables, these findings have inferential priority. More will be said on the relations between variables in Chapter 5, which discusses how main effects and interactions are interpreted in research reviews.

STUDY-GENERATED AND
REVIEW-GENERATED EVIDENCE

There are two different sources of evidence about relations contained in research reviews. The first type is called *study-generated evidence*. Specifically, study-generated evidence is present when a single study contains results that directly test the relation being considered. Research reviews also contain evidence that does not come from individual studies, but rather from the variations in procedures across studies. This type of evidence, called review-generated evidence, is present when the results of studies using different procedures to test the same hypothesis are compared to one another.

Any relation can be examined through either study- or review-generated evidence, but only study-generated evidence allows the reviewer to make statements concerning causality. An example will clarify the point. With regard to hyperactivity studies, suppose a reviewer is interested in whether stimulants and nonstimulants have different effects on hyperactivity. Suppose also that 16 studies are found that randomly assigned children to stimulant or nonstimulant experimental conditions. The accumulated results of these studies could then be interpreted as supporting or not supporting the idea that different drugs cause different effects on hyperactivity. Now assume that the reviewer uncovered 8 studies that employed only stimulant drugs tested against no-drug control groups and 8 other studies that compared only nonstimulant drugs with no-drug controls. If this review-generated evidence revealed a diminution in hyperactivity in the stimulant drug studies but not in the nonstimulant drug studies, then an association, but not a causal relation, could be inferred.

Why is this the case? Causal direction is not the problem with review-generated evidence. It would be foolish to argue that the amount of change in hyperactivity experienced by children caused the experimenters' choice of a drug. However, another ingredient of causality, the absence of potential third variables causing the relation, or nonspuriousness, is problematic. A multitude of third variables are potentially confounded with the original experimenter's choice of a stimulant or a nonstimulant drug. For instance, the experimenters who used nonstimulant drugs may also have employed different means for assessing hyperactivity. If the number of studies showing different results is large, it may be difficult to find other design characteristics confounded with the researchers' choice of what drug to use, but it is still possible. Therefore review-generated evidence cannot legitimately rule out variables confounded with the study characteristic of interest as possible true causes. Spuriousness cannot be eliminated because the reviewer did not randomly assign drugs to experiments! In primary research it is this random assignment that allows us to assume all third variables are represented equally in the experimental conditions.

The above example illustrates how review-generated evidence is typically used to examine potential moderators of relations. Like this example, most review-generated evidence examines interactional hypotheses, or the effect of a third variable on the strength or direction of a relation. It is often quite difficult to test main effect relations with review-generated evidence because social scientists use different scales to measure their dependent variables, even within a topic area. The problem of nonstandard measurements is circumvented when study characteristics are tested as *third* variables because the main effect relations *within* the studies can be transformed into standard effect size estimates, thus controlling for different scales (see Chapter 5).

One example of how main effect relations can be tested through review-generated evidence, however, is contained in the illustrative review of research design effects on response rates. In this review, studies were identified in which a particular design characteristic—say the employment of a monetary incentive—was experimentally manipulated by the primary researchers. That is, in some studies a randomly chosen subsample of potential respondents was given a monetary incentive and another subsample was not given an incentive. This is study-generated evidence on a main effect hypothesis. However, the reviewers were also able to locate studies that explicitly stated that *all* respondents received a monetary incentive or that *no* respondents received a monetary incentive. Because the dependent variables used in these studies were identical (i.e., response rates), it was possible to compare the response rates in these separate studies with one another, thus testing a main effect relation with review-generated evidence. The study-generated evidence comparing monetary incentive and no-incentive conditions could tell whether monetary incentives caused a difference in response rates. Such information could then be supplemented by examining the response rates in studies without an incentive and studies with an incentive. The second source of evidence could not stand alone as the basis of causal inferences, however.

It is important, then, for reviewers to keep the distinction between study-generated and review-generated evidence in mind. Only evidence coming from experimental manipulations within a single study can support assertions concerning causality. But the lesser status of review-generated evidence with regard to causal inferences does not mean this evidential base should be ignored. The use of review-generated evidence allows the reviewer to test relations which may have never been examined by primary researchers. Even though this evidence is equivocal, it is a major benefit of research reviewing and a source of potential hypotheses for future primary research.

THE ROLE OF PAST REVIEWS

If the topic of a review has a long history of interest within a discipline, it is likely that a reviewer attempting to use the guidelines set forth in this book will find that relevant reviews already exist. Obviously these efforts need to be scrutinized carefully before the new review is undertaken. Past reviews can help establish the necessity of a new review. This assessment process is much like that used in primary research before undertaking a new study.

There are several things a new reviewer can look for in past reviews. First, past reviews can be employed to identify the positions of other scholars in the field. In particular, past reviews can be used to determine whether conflicting conclusions exist about the evidence and, if they do, what has caused the conflict.

Second, a review of past reviews can assess the earlier efforts' completeness and validity. As a demonstration of the benefits of using quantitative procedures in reviews, this author (Cooper, 1979) compared a statistical review of research on gender differences in conformity to a traditional review (Maccoby & Jacklin, 1974). Using the same studies employed by the narrative reviewers, it was demonstrated that Maccoby and Jacklin's conclusions were somewhat conservative in light of the evidence they uncovered. Maccoby and Jacklin's analysis was also supplemented by a description of the magnitude of the gender-conformity relations.

Past reviews can also be a significant help in identifying interacting variables that the new reviewer might wish to examine. Rather than restart the compilation of potential moderating variables, past reviewers will undoubtedly offer many suggestions based on previous efforts and their own intellect. If more than one review of an area has been conducted, the new review will be able to incorporate all of the suggestions.

Finally, past reviews allow the researcher to begin the compilation of a relevant bibliography. Most reviews will have fairly lengthy bibliographies. If more than one review exists, their citations will overlap somewhat, but may also be quite distinct. As an example, Maureen Findley and this author (1981) found that the research cited under the same chapter titles in introductory social psychology textbooks differed substantially. Along with the techniques described in the next chapter, the research cited in past reviews provides an excellent place for the new reviewer to start the literature search.

The illustrative reviews. Of the four illustrative reviews, the review of locus of control and achievement is the one that best demonstrates the use of past reviews. Five previous reviews were located that made statements about the locus of control and achievement research evidence. Given that five past reviews existed, it was necessary to justify explicitly the need for a sixth review. First, it was claimed that only one of the past reviews looked at studies involving adult populations and this review did not examine age as a moderating variable. Thus the new review was the first to include all age groups. Second, the largest number of studies included in any past review was 36. By employing the techniques described in this book, 98 studies were found, meaning the new review was considerably more extensive than any of its predecessors. Third, two reviews were found that drew different conclusions on whether a student's gender influences the strength of the relation. Finally, across the five previous reviews there was considerable disparity in the language used to describe the strength of the locus of control-achievement relation. The new review would aid the interpretation of the relation by providing a mathematical estimate of the effect size. In general, then, the existence of five previous reviews was used not to diminish the importance of a sixth effort but to enhance it.

THE RESEARCH REVIEW CODING SHEET

Once the reviewer has formulated the problem and has an idea about what theorists, primary researchers, and past reviewers have said on the topic, the next step is to construct a coding sheet. The coding sheet is used to collect information from the primary research reports. If the number of studies involved in the research review is small, it may not be necessary for the reviewer to have a well-formulated idea about what information to extract from reports before the literature search begins. The relevant articles, if only a dozen or so exist, can be retrieved in their entirety and read and reread until the reviewer has gleaned the needed information. Small sets of studies allow the reviewer to follow up interesting ideas that emerge after several studies have already been read by returning briefly to previously scrutinized studies. However, if the reviewer expects to uncover a large amount of research, such a rereading of reports may be prohibitively time consuming. In this instance, it is necessary for the reviewer to consider carefully what data will be retrieved from each research report before the formal search begins. It is important to pilot test this expectation against a few research reports and to modify the coding sheet so that a fairly standard and through examination of each research report can be conducted in a single reading. The rules for constructing a coding sheet are similar to those used in creating a coding frame and data matrix for a primary research effort (see Selltiz et al., 1976).

The first rule in constructing a review coding sheet is that any information that might have the remotest possibility of being considered relevant to the research review should be retrieved from the studies. Once the literature search has begun, it is exceedingly difficult to re-retrieve forgotten information from already coded studies. It is much less of a problem to include mistakenly information that will not be used.

Information to include on the coding sheet. There are certain pieces of information about primary research that every reviewer will want to include on a research review coding sheet.

First, the reviewer will want to retrieve information concerning the background characteristics of the research report itself: the authors of the report, the source of the report, when the report was published, and what information channel led to the report's discovery.

The reviewer will also want to retrieve information concerning the design of the primary research. The particular design characteristics of interest will vary from topic to topic. Most areas involving experimental research will require information on how the dependent variable was measured and what operations were used to create empirically the independent variable. For personality or correlational studies, the reviewer will want to retrieve information concerning the names of the tests, whether they were standardized or unstandardized, the number of items they included, and perhaps the tests' reliabilities, if this information is available. We will return to the question of what aspects of research design need to be coded when the data evaluation stage of reviewing is discussed.

A third area of information needed in most reviews involves the characteristics of the participants included in the primary research. It is clearly important to retrieve the number of participants in the study. The reviewer will also want to retrieve information concerning the location and age of participants as well as any restrictions on participant populations that were employed.

Research review coding sheets should also contain information on the outcomes of the study. First and most important the coding sheet needs to identify the outcome of the comparison with regard to direction. Was the hypothesis supported, refuted, or a null result obtained? Was a third variable found that moderated a main effect? If a quantitative synthesis is envisioned, the reviewer will also need to record the statistical test employed and its associated magnitude, p-level, and degrees of freedom. If a measure of relationship strength was presented by the primary researchers, this should be of interest as well.

Each study report will also contain some miscellaneous but important design characteristics or results that the reviewer will want to note on the coding sheet. In many instances, the coding sheet will be standardized to accommodate information about the main effect comparison of interest, but the research report will contain evidence concerning interactions between the main effect and other variables. Therefore the coding sheet should contain space for noting the number of variables employed in a design or analysis and the outcomes of any interaction tests that involved the relation of interest.

The illustrative reviews. Of the four review examples, the most complex coding sheet was associated with the review of ethnic and social class differences in need for achievement. An example of this coding sheet is given in Figure 2.1

Along with the background information on the report itself, each coding sheet for this review left space for the identification of both an ethnic and social class comparison. The coders first identified each of the ethnic groups associated with the comparison. Each group then needed to be described separately with regard to its sample size and the gender, age, and location of participants. The initial pilot testing of the coding sheet revealed that any of the characteristics of the ethnic group samples could vary (along with ethnicity) between the two groups being compared.

The coding sheet then had space for the mean and standard deviation of each of the comparison groups on the need for achievement measure, as well as for a description of the inference test used to compare the groups. As might be expected, many of the reports did not give the mean and standard deviation of each group separately, so these lines were often left blank. In these cases, the line called "direction of results" was used to indicate which of the ethnic groups had the stronger need for achievement.

Social class information was also organized so as to identify two social class groups. Even though social class is a continuous measure, in nearly all

Author(s)_____

Title_____

Journal_____Year_____Vol._____Pgs_____

Source of Reference_____

1. Group 1　　　　　　　　　　　　　Group 2

　　Sex: Mn = _____ Fn = _____　　　Sex: Mn = _____ Fn = _____

　　Age_____　　　Age_____

　　Location_____　　　Location_____

　　Other restrictions_____　　　Other restrictions_____

2. Ethnic Group_____　　　Ethnic Group_____

　　Mean_____ sd _____　　　Mean_____ sd _____

　　　　Test_____ df error_____

　　　　Test value_____ df effect_____

　　　　p-level_____ effect size_____

　　Direction of results_____

3. Social class_____　　　Social class_____

　　Standardized_____Informal_____　　　Standardized_____Informal_____

　　How measured:　　　　　　　　　How measured:

　　　　Occupation_____　　　　Occupation_____
　　　　Salary_____　　　　Salary_____
　　　　Soc. status_____　　　　Soc. status_____

　　Mean_____ sd _____　　　Mean_____ sd _____

　　　　Test_____ df error_____

　　　　Test value_____ df effect_____

　　　　p-level_____ effect size_____

　　Direction of results_____

Figure 2.1: Coding Sheet for Studies of Ethnic Group and Social Class Differences in Need for Achievement

(continued)

4.   Dependent measures:

TAT (n-Ach)_____   Other_____

French's Test of Insight_____   _____

Ca. Psych. Inventory_____   _____

Figure 2.1: Continued

of the studies the social class comparison involved groups labelled middle class and lower class, often based on discrete indicators such as occupation of the father. The coders retrieved information on whether the measure of social class involved a standardized indexing system or some informal, researcher-developed system.

Next the coders retrieved information on the measurement of the dependent variable. Three of the most frequently used indexes of need for achievement were listed but space was left to describe other indexes. Several "homemade" tests of need for achievement were uncovered along with some tests of closely related constructs that were later judged for relevance (e.g., tests of future orientation, self-reliance).

Finally, although this is not shown in Figure 2.1, space was left for the coders to record the testing and significance of any interactions between ethnicity and social class, or any other variable that was of interest.

Each one of the coding sheets was designed to contain information concerning a single comparison. In some studies, comparisons were reported between more than two ethnic groups. For instance, a study might contain comparisons of need for achievement between whites, blacks, and Greeks. When such a study was uncovered, the coders would fill out separate sheets for each two-group comparison. Thus, a study with three ethnic groups would have three coding sheets associated with it. In Chapter 4 a more detailed discussion of how to identify independent comparisons will be presented.

VALIDITY ISSUES IN PROBLEM FORMULATION

Although several decisions during problem formulation that can affect the validity of a research review have been mentioned, the two most central involve the notions of conceptual breadth and operational detail.

First, reviewers who use only a few operational definitions in their reviews typically do so to ensure consensus about how their concepts are related to operations. Such agreement is an attractive scientific goal. However, most methodologists agree that multiple realizations of concepts are desirable. As stated above, if multiple operations produce similar results, numerous rival interpretations for the findings may be ruled out. Also narrow conceptualizations provide little information about the generality or robustness of a result. Therefore, the greater the conceptual breadth of a review, the greater its *potential* to produce conclusions that are more general than reviews using narrow definitions.

The word potential is emphasized because of the second threat to validity associated with the problem definition stage of review. If a reviewer only cursorily details study operations, the review conclusions may mask important distinctions in results. As Presby (1978) notes, "Differences (in studies) are cancelled in the use of very broad categories, which leads to the erroneous conclusion that research results indicate negligible differences in outcomes" (p. 514).

Of course, the most extreme attention to operational detail occurs when each study is treated as if it tested a completely different hypothesis. However, it is rare for a reviewer to conclude that no integration of the literature is possible, due to the variation in methods across studies. Therefore, most reviews contain some threat to validity from ignoring methodological differences between studies. But the risk occurs in varying degrees in different reviews.

A lack of overlap in the operational definitions considered relevant by different reviewers was not mentioned as a threat to validity, although it does create variance in review conclusions. This cannot be called a "threat," because it is impossible to say which of two reviews is more valid if the reviewers disagree about the operationalization of the same construct. Reviews which do not overlap in operations are not comparable on any level but the definitional one. On the other hand, it seems clear that a review which includes all the operations contained in another review plus additional operations is the more desirable review—if operational details receive appropriate treatment, of course. In practice, comparative evaluations will not be as clear-cut as these examples. Two reviews involving the same concept may share some operations while each also includes operations the other does not.

Protecting validity. Reviewers can use the following guidelines to protect their conclusions from the threats to validity entering during problem formulation:

(1) Reviewers should undertake their literature searches with the broadest possible conceptual definition in mind. They should begin with a few central operations but remain completely open to the possibility that other relevant operations will be discovered in the literature. When operations of questionable relevance are encountered, the reviewer should err toward making overly inclusive decisions, at least in the early reviewing stages.

(2) To complement conceptual broadness, reviewers should be exhaustive in their attention to the distinctions in study procedures. The slightest suspicion that a difference in study results is associated with a distinction in study methods should receive some testing by the reviewer, if only in a preliminary analysis.

EXERCISES

1. Identify two integrative research reviews that claim to review the same or similar hypotheses. Which review employs the broader conceptual definition? On what other dimensions concerning problem definition do the two reviews differ? What aspects of problem definition in each review do you find most helpful? (If you cannot find two related reviews, use the following: Bar-Tal & Bar Zohar, 1977; and Findley & Cooper, 1983.)

2. Identify a conceptual variable (e.g., "persistence" or "dogmatism") and list the operational definitions associated with it that are known to you now. Go to the library and find several reports that describe research relevant to your topic. How many new operational definitions did you find? Evaluate these with regard to their correspondence to the conceptual variable.

3. For studies on a topic of interest to you, draw up a preliminary coding sheet. Go to the library and find several reports that describe research relevant to the topic. How must you change the coding sheet to accomodate these studies? What did you leave out? (If you cannot think of a relation, use "gender differences in persistence.")

3

The Data Collection Stage

This chapter focuses on several methods for locating studies relevant to a review topic. Informal, primary, and secondary channels for obtaining research reports are described along with the biases that may be present in each channel. Background material for using four abstracting services is also presented. This chapter concludes with a discussion of threats to validity entering during data collection and ways to guard against them.

The major decision an inquirer makes during the data collection stage involves picking the *target population* that will be the referent for the inquiry (Williams, 1978). The target population includes those individuals, groups, or other elements that the inquirer hopes to represent in the study. A precise definition of a target population allows the researcher to list all of its constituent elements. Researchers are rarely required to generate such lists but because the truth or falsity of so many social science hypotheses depend on the elements of interest, it is important that researchers present clear general definitions. The *accessible population* includes those individuals, groups, or elements the inquirer is able pragmatically to obtain (Bracht & Glass, 1968). In most instances, researchers will not be able to access all of a target population's elements because it would be too costly to do so or because some elements are hard to find.

POPULATION DISTINCTIONS
IN SCIENTIFIC INQUIRY

Similarities between primary research and research review. Both primary research and research review involve specifying target and accessible populations. In addition, both types of inquiry require that the researcher consider how the target and accessible populations may differ from one another. To the extent that the elements in the accessible population are not representative of the target population, the trustworthiness of any claims about the target will be compromised. Because it is easier to alter the target of an investigation than it is to access hard-to-find elements, both primary researchers and research reviewers may find they need to restrict or respecify their target population once an inquiry is complete.

Differences between primary research and research reviews. The most general target population for primary social science research can be characterized roughly as "all human beings." Most subdisciplines, of course, respecify the elements to include less grandiose clusters, like all schizophrenics, all Americans, or all schoolchildren. Topic areas delineate targeted people even more specifically.

Accessible populations in social science research are typically much more restricted than targets. Indeed, in 1946, Quinn McNemar (1946) called psychology "the science of the behavior of sophomores" and this characterization remains largely accurate today (e.g., Findley & Cooper, 1981). Most social scientists are aware of the gap between the diversity of people they hope their research encompasses and those people actually accessible to them. In fact, this problem is so pervasive that most research journals do not require repeated attention to the difficulty in every research report.

As noted in the introductory chapter, research reviews involve two targets. First, the reviewer hopes the review will cover "all previous research" on the problem. Reviewers can exert some control over this goal through their choice of information sources. The next several sections of this chapter are devoted to what these sources are and how they are used. Second, the reviewer wants the results of the review to pertain to all the elements of interest in the topic area. The reviewer's influence is constrained at this point by the types of individuals who were sampled by primary researchers. Research reviewing thus involves a peculiar process of sampling samplers. The primary researcher samples individuals and the reviewer retrieves researchers. This process is something akin to cluster sampling (Williams, 1978) with the clusters distinguishing people according to the research projects in which they participated. In reality, reviewers typically are *not* trying to draw representative samples of studies from the literature. Instead, they attempt to retrieve an *entire* population of studies. This formidable goal is rarely achieved, but it is certainly more feasible in a review than in primary research.

METHODS FOR LOCATING STUDIES

This section will present some background on the major channels for locating studies. In addition, an attempt will be made to evaluate the kind of information in each channel by comparing its contents to that of "all relevant work," or to the entire population of relevant material the reviewer would find of interest. Regrettably, there is little empirical data on how the contents of different channels differ from each other or from all relevant work, so the comparisons will be speculative. The problem is complicated, of course, by the fact that the effect of the channel on its contents probably varies from topic to topic.

Informal Channels

The first informal source of information available to reviewers is their own research. The primary research that reviewers have conducted personally often has a strong, and perhaps overweighted, impact on their thinking (see Cooper, 1983).

Personal research will differ from all relevant research to the extent that the research outcomes are affected by the researcher's expectations. Individual researchers are also likely to employ repeatedly the same operations, causing many operational definitions relevant to a topic area to go unexamined in any particular laboratory.

The second informal source is the "invisible college" (Price, 1966). Invisible colleges, according to Crane (1969), are formed because "scientists working on similar problems are usually aware of each other and in some cases attempt to systematize their contacts by exchanging reprints with one another" (p. 335). Through a sociometric analysis, Crane found that most members of invisible colleges are not directly linked to one another but are linked to a small group of highly influential members. In terms of group communication, invisible colleges are structured like wheels—influential researchers are at the hub and less established researchers are on the rim, with lines of communication running mostly to the hub and less often among peripheral members.

Also, according to Crane (1969), invisible colleges are temporary units that deal with special problems and then vanish when the problem is solved or the focus of the discipline shifts. While estimates vary greatly from study to study, there is no doubt that researchers spend a significant amount of their time in informal exchanges through invisible colleges (Parker & Paisley, 1966).

The structure of invisible colleges and the influence of prominent and active researchers over the information contained in them hints at the biases in the information transmitted through invisible college links. Relative to all of the research that might be ongoing in a topic area, information from an invisible college is probably more uniformly supportive of the findings of the central researchers than evidence based on more diverse sources. For instance, a fledgling researcher who produces a result somewhat in conflict with the hub of an invisible college network is not likely to find that transmitting the result to the central researcher will mean widespread dissemination throughout the network. Disconfirming findings may lead a researcher to leave the network. Also, because the participants in an invisible college use one another as a reference group, it is likely that the kinds of operations and measurements employed in the members' research will be more homogeneous than that employed by all researchers who might be interested in a given topic.

A third source of information, bridging the distinction between formal and informal channels, is through attendance at professional meetings. A multitude of professional societies, structured both by career concerns and topic interests, exist within the social sciences and many of them hold yearly conventions at which papers are presented. By attending these meetings or requesting reprints, a researcher can discover what research others in their topic area are conducting and what research has recently been completed but has not yet entered the formal communication domain. In comparison to personal research and invisible colleges, the work found in convention programs is least likely to reveal a restricted sample of results or operations.

All of the informal channels share another important characteristic. Informal communications are more likely than formal ones to contain some inferior studies that have not been scrutinized carefully and that, because of methodological flaws, probably will not appear in more public systems. This is true of convention papers even though they do undergo evaluation because they are typically selected for presentation on the basis of very short descriptions.

A research reviewer who relies solely on informal channels to collect relevant work would be similar to a survey researcher who decided to sample only his or her friends. Given their obvious biases, it is surprising to find how large a role informal channels play in the research retrieval process. A study by Wood (1971) revealed that people interested in obtaining scientific information thought informal discussion was either the first or second most useful source of information. This preference was based primarily on the ease of informal communications. Most troubling is Wood's conclusion that "the quality of the channel has no bearing on the frequency with which the source is used" (p. 14).

Primary Channels

Primary publications form the initial link between the reviewer and the formal communication system. There are essentially two methods through which a potential reviewer gains access to primary works. First, reviewers can learn of research done in a topic area through the use of their personal libraries or the journals they regularly follow that are carried by their institutional library. The Report of the National Enquiry into Scientific Communication (1979) found that the average scholar in the humanities and several social science disciplines scanned approximately seven journals and followed four or five other journals on a regular basis. Most scholars said they spent between 10 and 12 hours per week reading scholarly books and journals and that this reading material came largely from their personal subscriptions.

The number of journals available and the amount of research being conducted has probably introduced some serious biases toward using personal libraries as the sole or major source of work for research reviews. As Garvey and Griffith (1971) noted, somewhere in the last information doubling period individual scholars lost the ability to keep abreast of all information relevant to their specialties through personal readings and journal subscriptions. This would not be a serious problem *if* the journals read by each researcher were a random sample of all journals available. However, researchers tend to operate within networks of journals. These journal networks, according to Xhignesse and Osgood (1967), involve a small number of journals which tend to cite other work available in the same journal and a small group of other outlets which also tend to cite one another. Xhignesse and Osgood found that about 30% of the citations in a given journal were to other work that appeared in the same journal and about 37% of citations were to other journals in the same network.

Given that personal libraries are likely to include journals in the same network, it would not be surprising to find some biases associated with the phenomenon. As with the more informal invisible colleges, we would expect greater homogeneity in both research findings and operations within a given journal network than in all the research available on a topic area. Again, however, the appeal of using the personal library and the journal network as a source of information lies in its ease of accessibility and its credibility to the reference group the reviewer hopes will read the review.

A second retrieval channel that uncovers primary publications is called the ancestry approach. Using this procedure, the reviewer retrieves information by tracking the research cited in already obtained relevant research. Most reviewers are aware of several studies bearing on their topic before they formally begin the literature search. These studies provide bibliographies which cite earlier related research. The reviewer can examine these citations and judge them for their relevance to the problem. The reference lists of cited articles can also be scrutinized. Through reiteration, reviewers work their way back through a literature until either the important concepts disappear or the studies become so old that the reviewer judges their results to be obsolete.

Searching study bibliographies is also likely to overrepresent work that appears within the reviewer's primary network of journals. Researchers tend to cite other work available through the same outlet or a small group of other outlets. We should therefore expect more homogeneity among references found through reference-tracking than would be present in all retrievable studies.

Both means for identifying studies through primary publications—personal libraries and the ancestry approach—share another bias. Obviously, published studies and studies found in their bibliographies are likely to overrepresent published research. However, the criteria for whether or not a study is published is not based solely on the scientific merit of the work. First, published research is probably biased toward statistically significant findings. This bias occurs primarily because of the practices and beliefs of researchers. Greenwald (1975) found that if a research project included a rejection of the null hypothesis the researcher intended to submit the result for publication about 60% of the time. On the other hand, if the study failed to reject the null hypothesis the researcher intended to submit the research for publication only 6% of the time. These intentions are probably based on the researcher's beliefs that nonsignificant findings are less interesting than significant ones and that journal editors are more likely to reject null results.

Also Nunnally (1960) noted that researchers whose findings conflict with the prevailing beliefs of the day are less likely to submit their results for publication than researchers whose work confirms presently held beliefs. Likewise, journal reviewers appear to look less favorably on studies that conflict with conventional wisdom than studies that support it. Bradley (1981) reported that 76% of university professors answering a mail questionnaire said they had encountered some pressure to conform to the subjective preferences of the reviewers of their work.

Along similar lines, Lane and Dunlap (1978) noted that the significance criteria for publication ensures that the size of differences reported in published works will be larger than the actual differences in the population of interest. As an empirical test of this phenomenon, Smith (1980) found 10 instances of research reviews in which the average size of a relation from published studies could be compared with the average relation in unpublished theses and dissertations. In all 10 instances, the relations in the published articles were larger than those in the theses and dissertations.

Primary publications, then, should not be used without convincing justification as the sole source of information for a research review. The use of personal libraries introduces bias by overrepresenting the paradigms and results that are contained in the reviewer's chosen journal network reference group. This bias will also be contained in the exclusive use of the ancestry, or reference-tracking, approach. In addition, both techniques will overrepresent published research and therefore introduce the biases associated with the tendency for journals to contain only statistically significant results and the pressure to conform to previous findings.

Secondary Channels

The channels of information called secondary sources should form the backbone of any systematic, comprehensive literature search. This is because secondary sources probably contain the information most closely approximating all publicly available research. These sources have the least restrictive requirements for a study to gain entry into the system.

Bibliographies are nonevaluative listings of books and articles that are relevant to a particular topic area. Often the topic areas are quite broad. Bibliographies are often maintained by single scientists or groups of individuals within a particular area, rather than by a formal organization. For instance, Carl White's *Sources of Information in the Social Sciences* (1973) lists bibliographies on topics such as suicide, psychoanalysis, and experimental aesthetics in psychology. It is also possible to find bibliographies of bibliographies. The Natural Research Council Research Information Service publishes a bibliography of bibliographies in psychology which lists over 2,000 bibliographies!

The use of bibliographies prepared by others can be a tremendous time-saver to a potential reviewer. The problem, however, is that the bibliographies are likely to be of much greater breadth than the reviewer's interest and they may still contain some of the biases discussed above. Also it is likely that most bibliographies will need updating for recent research. Even with these precautions, the use of bibliographies generated by others is strongly recommended because the compiler has spent many hours obtaining information and the biases involved in generating the bibliographies may obviate the biases that threaten the personal search of the reviewer.

The government system for publishing its own documents is a self-contained information retrieval system and might therefore be missed entirely by a researcher who does not decide to enter this system. Government documents fall into several categories—the most relevant to the present topic is called "research documents for specialists." Most government documents are printed by the Government Printing Office, which also issues a monthly catalogue that indexes the most recently published works. The novice entering the maze of government documents for the first time will probably find the *Guide to U.S. Government Publications* the best starting point. This work does not describe the documents themselves, but does describe the agencies that publish government documents.

In addition to federal government documents, state and local governments have published works that should be available in major research libraries.

Finally, the sources of information most likely to prove fruitful to the potential reviewer are the indexing and abstracting services associated with the social sciences. An index or abstracting service will focus on a certain discipline or topic area and define its scope to be an explicit number of primary publication outlets. Each article that appears in the primary outlets will then be referenced in the system.

The limitation of indexing and abstracting services is the long time lag, often three or four years, between when a study is completed and when it will appear in the system. Also, each service contains some restriction in what is allowed to enter the system, based on topical or disciplinary restrictions. For instance, *Psychological Abstracts* will include psychology-related journals (though certainly an exhaustive accounting of these) whereas the *Educational Research Information Center* will exhaustively contain education journals. Thus a reviewer interested in an interdisciplinary topic—like locus of control and achievement—needs to access more than one abstracting system. While secondary publications are least restrictive with regard to the studies within a discipline that will be contained in them, it is likely that more than one secondary source will be required for the literature search to be exhaustive.

ABSTRACTING AND INDEXING SERVICES

Two reasons were given above for why a single abstracting service probably cannot provide an exhaustive bibliography on many topics: (1) abstracting services tend to focus on particular disciplines but research questions are often interdisciplinary and (2) it typically takes from one to two years for a published report to appear in the abstracting services. A final limitation on the exhaustiveness of abstracting services derives not from their content but from how they are organized. Even though a service may cover exhaustively the journals that are relevant to a topic, searchers will not necessarily be able to describe their topic in a manner that will ensure they are able to uncover every relevant article, because the searcher must enter the abstracting service by specifying keywords associated with particular pieces of research. If a searcher is unaware of certain indexing terms that are applied to relevant articles or if the indexers omit terms that the searcher employs it is likely that some relevant articles will be missed. This problem will become clearer when the particulars of several abstracting services are discussed.

Psychological Abstracts. The most familiar and frequently used abstracting service in the behavioral sciences is *Psychological Abstracts.* This service covers literally every major journal in the world involved with psychology and related fields. *Psychological Abstracts* publishes monthly nonevaluative summaries of psychology articles along with author and subject indexes. Each monthly volume can include as many as 2,300 entries from journals, dissertations, and books. Abstracts are typically written by the authors of the articles themselves but indexing terms are applied by *Psychological Abstracts* employees. Twice a year a volume index is published which provides an expanded subject and author index for the preceding six months. Each volume is divided into 16 major classifications, including general psychology, psychometrics, developmental, social and experimental psychology, physical and psychological disorders, and educational and applied psychology.

The broad classifications give searchers their first opportunity to screen out potentially irrelevant articles. The major screening, however, begins with the searcher's use of the *Psychological Abstracts' Thesaurus of Psychological Terms.* The *Thesaurus* is much like a dictionary. It compiles the most recent vocabulary used to define psychological terms of present and past interest. Thus before a searcher can enter the *Psychological Abstracts,* he or she needs to have at least one term known to be used frequently to describe research in the area of interest. With this term, the searchers can find other

relevant terms by referring to the "Relationship" section of the *Thesaurus.*
The "Relationship" section displays the term that the searcher is aware of
and then lists other terms of either a broader or narrower range in the same
or related fields that have been used by the indexers to categorize studies.
Thus from a single term the searcher can expand the pool of potentially
relevant terms into related areas. For instance, the illustrative review examining the relation between locus of control and academic achievement
might have started with the searcher going to the "Relationship" section in
the *Thesaurus* and looking up the term "locus of control." Figure 3.1 reproduces the *Thesaurus's* entry for the term "internal-external locus-of-
control."

With an appropriate set of terms in hand, the searcher then goes to the
volume indexes. The searcher looks up in the subject index each of the terms
suggested by the *Thesaurus.* Under each term, the searcher finds a separate
entry for each abstract assigned to it, with all other terms that were used to
index each article that contained the term of interest. At the end of this
string of descriptors appears an abstract number, which is used by the
searcher to locate the full abstract for the particular article in the "Abstracts" section of the volume. Figure 3.1 also contains examples of an entry
in the subject index and an abstract.

The abstract itself can be retrieved and this fuller (but still short) description used to judge whether the article is relevant. Finally, if the abstract
proves interesting, its listing of the author(s), journal, and date of publication can be used to retrieve the full report.

The Educational Resources Information Center. The Educational Resources Information Center (ERIC) provides a multitude of information services for both practitioners and researchers. The ERIC system collects,
screens, organizes, and disseminates any literature associated with educational practices or issues. ERIC maintains 16 clearinghouses throughout the
country, each focusing on a different facet of education (e.g., adult education, reading, science education).

The ERIC system also has an associated dictionary called the *Thesaurus
of ERIC Descriptors.* Like *Psychological Abstracts,* these descriptors are
used to index and enter documents into the ERIC system and to assist users
in retrieving documents relevant to their search. In addition to the *Thesaurus,* ERIC publishes two monthly guides to its contents. The first of interest
to us here is *Resources in Education (RIE).* It presents the abstracts to
recently completed research reports and other documents of educational
significance. These are indexed by subject, author, institutional source, and
the type of publication (e.g., journal article, book, convention paper). The
second guide is called the *Current Index to Journals in Education.* It
presents a monthly listing of the periodical literature covering more than

A. Relationship Section Entry for Internal-External Locus of Control in the *Thesaurus of Psychological Terms*

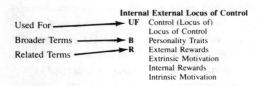

B. Subject Index Entry (partial) for Internal-External Locus of Control (July-Dec 1981)

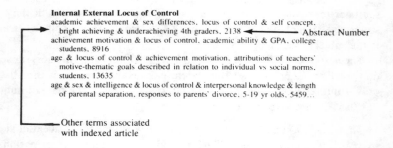

C. Abstract Entry for Abstract Number 2138 (July 1981)

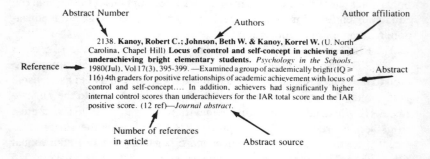

SOURCE: Used by permission of the American Psychological Association.

Figure 3.1: Examples of Entries in *Psychological Abstracts*

700 major educational and education-related publications. Most documents stored in *RIE* can be retrieved in their entirety through the system. The full documents are typically contained in microfiche collections which can be found in major research libraries.

The steps involved in the use of *RIE* parallel those of the *Psychological Abstracts*. First, the searcher consults the *Thesaurus of ERIC Descriptors,* organized like the *Thesaurus of Psychological Terms*. That is, the searcher provides key descriptors relevant to the search and the *Thesaurus* then helps identify broader, narrower, and related terms which might be relevant. Figure 3.2 provides examples of *Thesaurus* and index entries for the term "locus of control." The searcher then consults the monthly issues of *Resources in Education* and the semi-annual indexes for a listing of relevant documents that appear in the volumes associated with each index term. Following these brief article descriptions in the subject index, an accession number appears which can be used to find either the abstract or full report. The *Current Index of Journals in Education* is entered in the same manner as *Resources in Education,* but the two guides need to be searched separately.

With the accession numbers in hand, the searcher goes to the "Resume" section in either of the guides to find the title, author, source, and abstract associated with the article. If the article is still deemed potentially relevant, the searcher proceeds to the microfiche collection which contains transparencies that can be placed on microfiche reading machines to bring the document to full size. It is then possible in many libraries to photocopy the magnified microfiche documents to obtain a paper copy of the document. Or the searcher can contact the ERIC Document Reproduction Service to obtain a copy.

Dissertation Abstracts International. While many abstracting services also contain abstracts of dissertations, *Dissertation Abstracts International (DAI)* focuses exclusively on the dissertation. However, *DAI* is broad in that all dissertations, regardless of discipline, are abstracted in it. Thus, the first job of the searcher is to identify those disciplines and subdisciplines that are of interest.

The materials in *DAI* are indexed according to author and important keywords in the dissertation title. No indexer reads each dissertation in order to assign descriptive terms. Instead, a dissertation will appear in *DAI's* subject indexes only under those important words that appear in the dissertation title. Also, *DAI's* cumulative volumes contain only the abstracts associated with the dissertation. Few libraries maintain microfilm copies of the complete dissertations and therefore, when an abstract appears relevant, the searcher usually must contact University Microfilms in order to obtain a full-length copy of the dissertation.

A. Alphabetic Descriptor Display Entry for Locus of Control in the *Thesaurus* of ERIC Descriptors

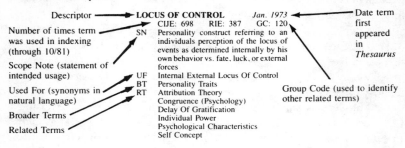

B. Subject Index Entry for Locus of Control in *Resources in Education* (July 1982)

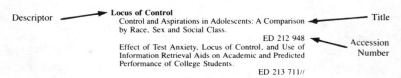

C. Document Resume (partial) for Accession Number ED 213 711 (July 1982)

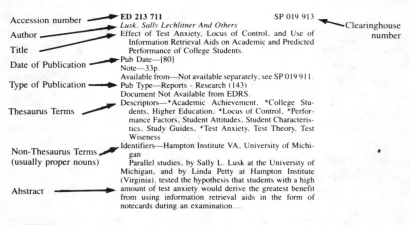

SOURCE: Used by permission of the Educational Resources Information Center.

Figure 3.2: Examples of Entries in ERIC

Obtaining dissertations is not only time consuming but it can also be very expensive. Reviewers might consider writing to dissertation authors and asking to borrow theses or copies of preprints or reprints of articles based on theses. Alternatively, the abstracts of dissertations are generally more detailed than those published in the *Psychological Abstracts* or *ERIC*. Therefore, it is sometimes possible for a searcher to glean from the abstract itself the information needed to use the dissertation in the research review, if only in a cursory fashion. Figure 3.3 presents some of the features of *DAI*.

The Social Sciences Citation Index. The Social Sciences Citation Index (SSCI) is a unique indexing service because it categorizes documents based on the work cited in it as well as its topical focus. According to the publishers of the SSCI, "a citation index for the journal literature identifies and groups together all newly published articles that have referenced (cited) the same earlier publication. The earlier publication becomes, in effect, an indexing term for current articles that deal with the same subject" (Institute for Scientific Information, 1980, p. 3). An example will make this strategy clear. At the beginning of the search for locus of control and achievement studies, the searchers might have been aware of several standard measures of locus of control. One such measure, called the Intellectual Achievement Responsibility (IAR) Scale, was developed by Virginia C. Crandall (Crandall, Katovsky, & Crandall, 1965). With this knowledge, the searchers could enter the SSCI by looking up "Crandall, V. C.," where they would find a listing of all articles for which "V. C. Crandall" was the first author that had been cited by other articles during the covered period. Each article that had cited a Crandall work would be listed by its author, source, and date of publication. Those articles citing Crandall's 1965 publication could have correlated the IAR scale with an academic achievement measure. A starting point for screening articles on this basis might be the SSCI Source Index. The Source Index lists publications making citations alphabetically, and contains the full title and bibliographical reference to the article, as well as a summary of the articles' citations. After the Source Index, the searcher can go directly to the full report. Figure 3.4 presents an example of a citation index entry.

Citation indexes are most useful when particular researchers or research papers are closely associated with a problem area. The searcher can retrieve studies which cite central researchers in an area and then screen these for topic relevance. Perhaps the most remarkable thing about the SSCI is the breadth of its social science coverage. The SSCI indexes every article in over 1,500 journals that cover 50 different social science disciplines. The SSCI selectivity covers nearly 3,000 other journals that might or might not have social science information in them. Through this process the SSCI compiles more than 130,000 new journal articles every year.

A. Keyword Title Index Entry for "Locus" (partial) *(Humanities and Social Sciences,* November 1981)

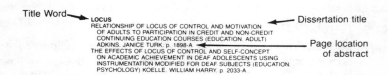

B. Dissertation Abstract (partial) from p. 2033-A *(Humanities and Social Sciences,* November 1981)

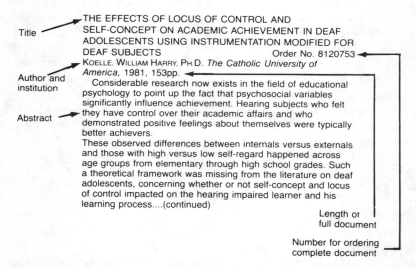

Figure 3.3: Examples of Entries in *Dissertation Abstracts International*

A. Citation Index Entry (partial) under Crandall, VC (1981, Annual)

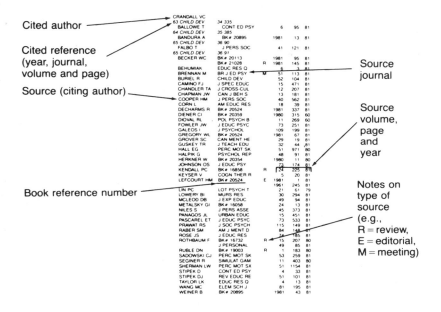

Cited author

Cited reference
(year, journal,
volume and page)

Source (citing author)

Book reference number

Source journal

Source volume, page and year

Notes on type of source (e.g., R = review, E = editorial, M = meeting)

B. Permuterm Index Entry for Locus-of-Control (1981, Annual)

Primary term

Co-terms

First author of article

Figure 3.4: Examples of Entries from _Social Sciences Citation Index_

The SSCI also contains a subject index, called the Permuterm Subject Index, which uses the significant words in article titles to index documents. Every significant title word is paired with every other significant title word creating a two-level indexing system. Thus a searcher can take a single term and find it in the Permuterm Index and then examine the paired terms that might prove relevant to the relation under study. This feature of the SSCI is also illustrated in Figure 3.4.

Space limitations make it impossible to examine each of the hundreds of abstracting services available in the social sciences. For a broad overview of these sources, the reader should consult Carl White's *Sources of Information in the Social Sciences* (1973). For more detailed descriptions of how to use the four abstracting services covered here, readers should consult their local reference librarian.

Computer searches. The social science indexing and abstracting services allow the searcher to access thousands of documents from a wide variety of sources. The systems' exhaustiveness, coupled with the explosion in social science research, however, do not solve the problem of information overload as much as they underscore it. The reader may have been struck by the time needed to conduct a comprehensive search of any of the four abstracting services, if a topic is broad. Without considerable time and money, it might appear that a thorough search of the abstracts is beyond the capability of a single searcher or even search team.

Luckily, the computer revolution has touched the scientific communication system and has greatly reduced the effort needed to accomplish an exhaustive literature search. Instead of spending many hours manually searching the abstracting systems, the computer makes it possible to access several abstracting services in just one or two hours. Most major research libraries have on-line computer searches available. These can access literally hundreds of abstracting services that have been placed on computer tapes. The tapes are accessible through phone hookups to central computer storage facilities. For instance, the DIALOG/Information Retrieval Service has been in use since 1972. The DIALOG system stores more than 200 abstracting services and contains more than 35 million records.

It is not necessary for the searcher to know how to operate the computer to use the computer search services. Research libraries employ trained specialists who conduct the actual search once they have the needed information from the searcher. Typically, the searcher tells the librarian the topic of interest and most importantly, what terms, synonyms, and related terms are involved in the search. The librarian and the searcher can browse through the thesauri to identify terms that the searcher might not have considered initially. Searchers are also often asked by the librarian to provide examples of documents they hope to retrieve to give some concrete idea about the material they desire.

Each of the four abstracting services described above has a slightly different technique for retrieval through the computer. For instance, the *Psychological Abstracts* can be accessed using several different computer retrieval techniques. First, the *Thesaurus* can be used to identify "descriptor fields." That is, as noted above, every document included in *Psychological Abstracts* has been read by an indexer and assigned a series of terms (taken from the *Thesaurus*) that describe the document's contents. Documents can then be retrieved by asking the computer to identify those that have been assigned the relevant descriptors. It takes the computer only seconds to tell how many documents have been assigned a descriptor and to print out examples of the documents covered.

A second technique is to use "natural language" or "free text" to identify terms that appear in the article title or abstract. The use of natural language descriptors frees the librarian and searcher from relying on the *Thesaurus* and the judgment of the indexer for identifying documents that might be relevant. This technique is especially useful if the searcher is interested in finding new terms that have not found their way into the *Thesaurus*.

A third method is to use the "identifier field." The identifier field contains, among other significant phrases, the proper nouns that appear in a document. For example, a searcher interested in examining the literature relevant to the "Hawthorne effect" would not find the term "Hawthorne effect" in the *Thesaurus*. However, because it is a proper noun, the identifier field can be used to search for all documents that mention the Hawthorne effect. The identifier field is also useful when a searcher wants to find research involving a particular test (e.g., the WISC or Strong Vocational Inventory).

Finally, *Psychological Abstracts* can be searched via the computer by using author names, journals, or institution. If the searcher is interested in obtaining all of the research conducted at the Center for Research in Social Behavior, this institutional name could be used to locate relevant documents.

Psychological Abstracts is available on computer tape from the present back to 1967. In some instances, the searcher may be interested in older documents, and these would have to be retrieved manually. Interestingly, however, the computerized abstracts are more up to date than the printed volumes available on the library shelves, because the process of abstracting and indexing articles is now done directly onto computer tape, which then generates the printed volumes.

The computerized ERIC system is similar to *Psychological Abstracts,* although of course, it has its own thesaurus. Also the ERIC descriptor or index terms are divided into major and minor categories. Thus searchers have the option of retrieving only those studies in which the important terms are a major focus in the document or including those documents that treat their interest only tangentially. The other three means of accessing the system—use of free text, identifiers, and authors, journals, or institutions— are also available with ERIC. The ERIC data base is computerized back to the year 1966.

Dissertation Abstracts International has a much less sophisticated means for computerized retrieval. Documents can be located only through the use of free text terms that appear in dissertation titles. It is possible, however, to circumscribe the search somewhat by requesting that the computer access only a broad subject area. For instance, if the searcher is interested in psychological studies examining the Hawthorne effect, "Hawthorne effect" could be used as the keyword and the computer could be requested to only retrieve studies that appeared in the psychology subject category. It is also possible to search *Dissertations Abstracts International* through the use of the dissertation author or the institution granting the degree.

Dissertation abstracts (from *Dissertation Abstracts International, American Doctoral Dissertations,* and *Comprehensive Dissertation Index*) have been computerized back to the year 1861.

Subject searches of the Social Science Citation Indexes can be accomplished only through the use of free text terms from article titles. Subject searches can be specified to include only a specific type of document such as journal articles, news reports, or book reviews. In order to use the citation index component of SSCI, the searcher must provide the reference whose citation history is of interest. A problem with the use of the citation indexes is that numerous errors are contained in the bibliographic information included in journal articles (Boyce & Banning, 1979). Apparently authors and editors spend little time proofreading references so it is often necessary for searchers to retrieve general information on a cited author and then sift through them to identify citations that are not listed accurately. Of course, this is a problem for the manual searcher of SSCI as well as for the computerized searcher. The SSCI has been computerized back to 1972.

The monetary cost of running a computer search is not prohibitive. In fact, approximately 90% of the searches run in this author's research library cost between $10 and $30, with ERIC searches the least expensive and SSCI searches the most expensive.

After meeting with the librarian and interacting with the computer, the searcher can request a printed bibliography that includes the authors, references, titles, and abstracts of every potentially relevant article. These bibliographies are sent through the mail by the computer services and usually arrive less than a week after the search. Bibliographies can also be printed "on line," but at much greater expense.

It is impossible to overemphasize the value of the computer search to the research reviewer. The reviewer obtains an exhaustive listing of potentially relevant documents with phenomenal speed. Because of the amount of time saved and the convenience of having a hard copy of the search outcome, which can then be evaluated at the reviewer's convenience, the search can be much broader than if it were undertaken manually.

Computer searching is not without problems. In particular, when the computer is used, keywords must be completely specified before the search begins, eliminating the possibility of following up any promising leads that might arise during the search (Menzel, 1966; Stoan, 1982). If computerized searches precluded manual searches, the loss of accidental discoveries would be troubling indeed. However, the searcher is still free to browse and browsing is recommended before the computer search begins. Not only can browsing expand the searcher's keywords for the computer but the searcher can identify relevant articles which should appear on the computer printout. If they do not appear, something has gone awry.

Finally, there is empirical evidence that computer searching has some beneficial by-products. In an experimental study, Feinberg (1981) assigned students to either a "standard bibliographic skills" group or a computer search group for doing term papers. He found students in the computer search group received higher grades, believed the library was more adequate for literature reviews, and derived more satisfaction from the assignment than students who used standard bibliographic procedures.

DETERMINING THE ADEQUACY OF LITERATURE SEARCHES

The question of which and how many sources of information to use has no general answer. The appropriate sources will be a function partly of the topic under consideration and partly of the resources of the reviewer. As a rule, however, I suggest that searchers should always employ multiple channels so that the chances of a strong unidentified bias distinguishing included from unincluded studies is small. If a reviewer has uncovered different studies through channels that do not share similar biases, then the overall conclusions of the review should be replicable by another reviewer using different, but also complementary, sources for primary research. This rule embodies the scientific criterion of replicability.

Informal sources revisited. Earlier in this chapter it was stated that the information contained in informal channels is not likely to reflect information gleaned from all potential sources. This research, however, was also shown to complement that gained through formal channels because it is likely to be more recent. Therefore searchers should not exclude it but should carefully examine the percentage of the total relevant literature that is made up of information retrieved through informal sources. If this percentage is large, searchers should go to other secondary sources before terminating the search.

Published versus unpublished research. It was also mentioned earlier that concentrating on only published research will produce a set of studies that overemphasize significant results. However, it may be counterargued that published research has undergone the most rigorous methodological appraisal by established researchers and probably is of the highest quality.

A focus on only published research might be legitimate in two circumstances. The first is when the published research contains several dozen, or in some cases hundreds, of relevant works. In such an instance it is likely that while the published research may overestimate the magnitude of a relation, it probably will not incorrectly identify relation direction. The suggested magnitude of the relation can be cautiously interpreted. Also, enough instances of a hypothesis test will be covered to allow a legitimate examination of which study characteristics covary with study outcomes.

Second, there are many hypotheses that have multiple testings in the literature which were *not* the primary focus of the research. For instance, many psychological and educational studies include gender as a variable in the research design and report hypothesis tests of gender differences, although these are only an ancillary interest of the primary researchers. The bias toward significant results in publications probably does not extend much beyond the primary hypothesis. Therefore a hypothesis that appears in many articles as a secondary interest of the researchers will be affected by the publication bias to a lesser degree than the researcher's primary focus.

The illustrative reviews. For the review of the relation between locus of control and academic achievement, the on-line computer search included *Psychological Abstracts,* ERIC, and *Dissertation Abstracts International.* The keywords used as both descriptors and free text identifiers were a crossing (intersection) of the terms "achievement" or "performance" with the terms "locus of control" or "internal-external." The computer located 802 studies which mentioned both of these terms in either their title or abstract, or were described by both terms by the indexers. Using the abstracts provided by the computer service, the researchers reduced the 802 references to 208 still considered potentially relevant. Of these, references appearing in *Psychological Abstracts* and ERIC were examined in their entirety while only the abstracts of dissertations were inspected. Ultimately, 98 relevant studies were retrieved. These 98 studies contained 275 tests of the hypothesis. Given the size of the sample and the fact that it was already nearly three times larger than the sample used in the next most exhaustive review, none of the other techniques for identifying relevant articles were employed.

The literature search for the review of how research design affects response rates to questionnaires was quite different. *Psychological Abstracts, SSCI, BRS/Inform,* and *Management Contents* were used as parts of the computerized abstract search with the keywords "response rate," "inducement," "incentive," "survey," or "questionnaire." This search, as the descriptors indicate, was one for which the computer was least effective in uncovering relevant research. The reason, of course, was the difficulty in generating a list of descriptors that captured adequately the nature of the hypothesis under study. The computer uncovered 98 citations and of these 25 were ultimately deemed relevant. Not surprisingly, however, a tracking of the references mentioned in these 25 articles (and past reviews) revealed an additional 68 relevant studies. Thus a total of 93 relevant articles were obtained which included 497 response rates that could be associated with different techniques. The literature search was also restricted to research which had been conducted after 1965. The age-of-research restriction was employed because it was felt that research previous to 1965 might not reflect accurately the response habits of present-day populations.

Without going into detail, the search for studies examining ethnic and social class differences in achievement motivation revealed 42 studies that each contained at least one relevant comparison and the drug-treatment-of-hyperactivity search found 61 relevant studies.

VALIDITY ISSUES IN STUDY RETRIEVAL

At the beginning of this chapter, it was mentioned that literature searches have two different targets—previous research and individuals or elements relevant to the topic area. It is necessary therefore for research reviewers to address the adequacy of their accessed studies with respect to each of the targets. The reviewer must ask (1) how the retrieved studies might differ from all studies and (2) how the elements contained in retrieved studies might differ from all elements of interest. Much of this chapter has dealt with how to answer the first of these questions. Every study does not have an equal chance of being retrieved by the reviewer. It is likely that studies contained in the reviewer's retrieval channels are different from studies that never become public or that can be accessed through other channels. Therefore, the reviewer must pay careful attention to what the inaccessible studies might have to say and how this might differ from what is contained in studies that have been retrieved.

The reviewer's second population of interest, referring to individuals or other basic units of analysis, injects a note of optimism into the discussion. There is some reason to believe research reviews will pertain more directly to an area's target population than will the separate primary research efforts in the topic area. The overall literature can contain studies conducted at different times, on adults and children, and in different countries with varied racial and ethnic backgrounds (as well as under different testing conditions with different methods). For certain problem areas containing numerous replications, the population of referent individuals accessible to a reviewer may closely approximate the target population of the primary researcher. While a resignation to population restrictions in primary research is understandable, we need not be so acquiescent about the referent population of research reviews. We must bear in mind, of course, that the bias against null and contradictory findings may affect the available samples of elements as well as the sampled studies of the review. To the extent that more retrievable studies are associated with particular subpopulations of elements, the retrieval bias will restrict the accessible populations of individuals.

The first threat to validity associated with the data-gathering phase is that the studies in the review probably will not include all studies pertinent to the topic of interest. Again, reviewers should access as many information channels as needed to ensure that no obvious, avoidable bias exists, within the limits set by cost effectiveness.

The second threat to validity occurring during study retrieval is that the individuals or elements in the retrieved studies may not represent all individuals or elements in the target population. Of course, the primary researcher's choice of units is beyond the control of the research reviewer, but the reviewer is obligated to describe carefully the missing populations and to qualify any conclusions based on missing or overrepresented samples.

Protecting Validity

1. The most crucial protection against threats to validity caused by inadequate data collection comes from a broad and exhaustive search of the literature. While the law of diminishing returns does apply here, a complete literature search has to include at least one major abstracting service, informal communications, and the bibliographies of past research or reviews. The more exhaustive a search, the more confident a reviewer can be that another reviewer using many but perhaps not identical sources of information will reach a similar conclusion.

2. In their manuscripts, reviewers should be explicit about how studies were gathered, including information on sources, years, and keywords covered in the search. Without this information, the reader of the review has no way of comparing the validity of a particular review's conclusion with the conclusions that may be contained in other reviews.

3. Reviewers should present whatever indices of potential retrieval bias are available to them. For instance, Rosenthal and Rubin (1982) distinguished published research from dissertations to determine if the evidence from the two sources differed. Cooper, Burger, and Good (1981) reviewed only published studies but speculated that little publication bias was present in their conclusions because the report titles rarely mentioned the hypothesis of interest (i.e., gender differences in locus of control).

4. The research reviewer should summarize the sample characteristics of individuals used in the separate studies. Given the general gloom that accompanies most discussion of sample representativeness in the social sciences, many reviewers will find this practice reveals an unexpected strength rather than weakness in their research reviews.

EXERCISES

1. Count the number of abstracts indexed under the terms "cognitive dissonance" and "learned helplessness" in the yearly indexes to *Psychological Abstracts* from 1965 to the present. What does this tell you about research in these two areas? What does it tell you about the completeness of *Psychological Abstracts* listings on these two topics?

2. Define a topic area by specifying the keywords (and their crossings or intersections) that would guide a literature search. Pick a few years and do a manual search of an abstract service to locate relevant artices. Perform a parallel computer search. How are the two outcomes different? Which one was more useful and cost-effective?

3. For a topic of your choice, choose the channels you would use to search the literature and the order in which you would access them. For each step in the search, describe its strengths, limits, and cost-effectiveness.

4

The Data Evaluation Stage

Three approaches to judging the methodological adequacy are detailed. Also discussed are problems encountered in retrieving data from studies and the procedures used to identify independent hypothesis tests when multiple tests or multiple studies are reported. The chapter concludes with a discussion of validity issues relevant to the data evaluation stage.

The data evaluation stage in a scientific endeavor involves making judgments about whether or not individual data points should be included in the inquiry. This activity must be carried out regardless of whether the data points are the scores of individuals or the outcomes of studies. Data evaluation requires the establishment of criteria for judging the procedural adequacy of how the data were generated. Inquirers must examine all of the potential influences on each data point that may make it irrelevant to the problem under consideration. Then they must determine whether these influences are substantial enough to require that the data point be dropped from the inquiry.

EVALUATIVE DECISIONS
IN SCIENTIFIC INQUIRY

Similarities between primary research and research review. Both primary researchers and research reviewers examine their data sets for wild values, errors in recording, or other unreliable measurements. In primary research, individual data points are compared to sample distributions to discover if they are so extreme as to be of questionable validity (that is, statistical outliers; see Barnett & Lewis, 1978). The search for statistical outliers in research review involves the examination of relationship magnitudes to determine if the strength of a relation in any study is too different from other studies to be considered reliable. Errors in recording are identified in both kinds of research through recalculation of results or the examination of wild values. A primary researcher may observe that a given individual's score is not on the scale of values employed for that particular variable. A research reviewer may recalculate the values of statistical tests presented in a study and find that the primary researcher's calculations were in error.

Differences between primary research and research review. Other means for identifying unreliable data are different for the two types of inquiry. In primary research, an individual's responses are sometimes discarded because surrounding evidence reveals the individual did not attend to the appropriate stimuli or that the response instructions were misunderstood (see Carlsmith et al., 1976). If deception or some other form of misdirection was used in the research, individual data may be discarded because the participant did not believe the cover story or deduced the hidden hypothesis.

In research review there is only one potential criterion (beyond discordancy and error) for discarding data: the validity of the study's methods. Reviewers decide whether each study was conducted in a careful enough manner so that the result can be trusted. Reviewers can make either a discrete decision—whether to include the study—or a continuous one—whether to weight studies dependent on their relative degree of trustworthiness. A large part of this chapter will be devoted to criteria for judging the methodological quality of a study.

Most social scientists agree that methodological quality should be the primary criterion for decisions about how much trust to place in a study's results. However, in practice the predispositions of reviewers about what the outcome of the review should be often have a strong impact on how studies are evaluated. It is important to examine the sources and effects of reviewers' prior beliefs.

PREDISPOSITIONS OF THE REVIEWER

Almost every primary researcher and research reviewer begins an inquiry with some idea about the outcome of the inquiry. In primary research, methodologists have constructed elaborate systems of controls to eliminate artifactual results created by experimenter expectancy effects (Rosenthal, 1976). In research reviews no such system of controls has been employed. Reviewers are fully aware of their biases *and* the outcomes of studies as the research is being evaluated. This leads to the possibility that the evaluation of research will be colored by its outcomes. The impact of predispositions on reviews has been so great that Gene Glass (1976) made the following remark about the process:

> A common method for integrating several studies with inconsistent findings is to carp on the design or analysis deficiencies of all but a few studies—those remaining frequently being one's own work or that of one's students or friends—and then advance the one or two "acceptable" studies as the truth of the matter (p. 4).

Mahoney (1977) called this "confirmatory bias" and he performed an experiment that directly tested the impact of predispositions on the evaluation of research. He samples guest editors for the *Journal of Applied Behav-*

and asked them to rate several aspects of a controlled manu-
~ney found that the methods, discussion, and contribution of the
were evaluated more favorably if the study confirmed the re-
disposition about the results. In a related study, Lord, Ross, and
9) found that readers rated pro-attitudinal studies as better con-
counter-attitudinal studies. More strikingly, the undergraduates
who participated in the Lord and colleagues study showed *polarization* in
attitudes despite the fact that they all read the same research abstracts. That
is, even though all participants read one study that supported their prior
belief and one that refuted it, after reading the two studies participants saw
more support for their initial positions.

It appears then that predispositions toward a review's results can influence the reviewers' judgments about the methodological quality of a piece
of research. If a study disconfirms the reviewer's predisposition, the reviewer is more likely to attempt to find some aspect of the study which
renders it irrelevant or methodologically unsound. On the other hand, studies that confirm the predisposition may be included although their relevance
is questionable or their methods seriously flawed.

JUDGING RESEARCH QUALITY

Problems with quality judgments may be even more extensive than those
associated with reviewer predispositions. It may be the case that even "disin-
terested" judges of research could not agree on what is and is not a quality
study.

Studies of evaluator agreement about research quality. Several studies
have examined the reliability of judgments made about manuscripts submitted to journals in the field of psychology. These studies typically calculate
the correlation between the recommendations made by manuscript readers
concerning whether or not a manuscript should be accepted for publication.
In many respects the judgments of manuscript evaluators are more complex
than those of research synthesizers. The manuscript evaluator must consider several dimensions that do not interest the research synthesizer, including the clarity of writing and the interests of the journal's readership.
Also, a journal editor will sometimes deliberately choose evaluators who
represent different perspectives. However, the editor still hopes that the
evaluators will agree on the disposition of the manuscript. And, of course, if
perfectly objective criteria were available (and were employed), the evaluators would come to concurring decisions.

The interclass correlations reported in studies of manuscript evaluators'
agreement on publication decisions range from $r = +.54$ (reported by Scarr
& Weber, 1978) to $r = +.19$ (reported by Cicchetti & Eron, 1979). Marsh and

Ball (1981) collected judgments on the "quality of research design and analysis" and found the interjudge reliability was $r = +.27$.

In an interesting demonstration, Peters and Ceci (1982) resubmitted 12 already-published research articles to the journals in which they initially appeared. The manuscripts were identical to the originals except that the names and institutions of the submitters were changed from "high status" to "low status." Only 3 of the 12 articles were detected as being resubmissions. Of the 9 articles that completed the re-review process, 8 were *not* accepted for publication. The journal in which the Peters and Ceci (1982) report appears, *The Behavioral and Brain Sciences,* contains open peer commentary on this study and peer review in general.

Some of the differences between judgments by manuscript evaluators and research synthesizers were controlled for in a study conducted by Gottfredson (1978). He removed much of the variability in judges' ratings, which might be due to differing initial biases, by asking authors to nominate experts competent to evaluate their work. Gottfredson was able to obtain at least two expert evaluations for each of 121 articles. The experts evaluated the quality of the articles on a 3-question scale which left the meaning of the term "quality" ambiguous. An interjudge agreement coefficient of $r = +.41$ was obtained. On a 36-item evaluation scale which tapped many explicit facets of research quality, an interjudge agreement coefficient of $r = +.46$ was obtained.

A judgment of the overall quality of a study requires the evaluator to assess and combine several dimensions along which studies can differ. It is therefore possible to locate two sources of variance in evaluators' decisions: (1) the relative importance they assign to different research design characteristics and (2) their judgments about how well a particular study met a design criterion. To demonstrate the first source of variance, I asked six experts in school desegregation research to rank order the importance of six design characteristics for establishing the "utility or information value" of a school desegregation study (Cooper, 1983). The six characteristics were (1) the experimental manipulation (or in this case, the definition of desegregation); (2) the adequacy of the control group; (3) the validity of the outcome measure; (4) the representativeness of the sample; (5) the representativeness of the environmental conditions surrounding the study; and (6) the appropriateness of the statistical analyses. The intercorrelations of the rankings among the experts varied from $r = +.77$ to $r = -.29$, with the average correlation being $r = +.47$.

In sum, the studies of evaluator agreement are somewhat disheartening. It should be pointed out, of course, that the reliability of judgments can be enhanced by adding more judges. That is, a decision to accept or reject an article for publication based on ten evaluators' ratings will, on average, correspond more with the consensus of ten other evaluators than any two evaluators' decisions. Rarely, however, are very large pools of evaluators used to make quality judgments about research by either journal editors or research synthesizers.

A priori exclusion of research versus a posteriori examination of research differences. The studies of agreement about research quality and the role of predispositions in the evaluation process demonstrate instances in which subjectivity intrudes on attempts to reach consensus about our world. The point is important because there is considerable disagreement about whether or not a priori judgments of research quality should be used to exclude studies from research reviews.

This debate was perhaps best captured in an exchange of views between Hans Eysenck (1978) and Gene Glass and Mary Smith (1978) concerning Smith and Glass's (1977) review of research on psychotherapy. Smith and Glass (1977) reviewed over 300 studies of psychotherapy with no a priori exclusion of studies due to poor methodology. Eysenck felt this strategy represents an abandonment of scholarship and critical judgment:

> A mass of reports—good, bad, and indifferent—are fed into the computer in the hope that people will cease caring about the quality of the material on which the conclusions are based. . . . "Garbage in—garbage out" is a well-known axiom of computer specialists; it applies here with equal force (p. 517).

Eysenck concluded that "only better designed experiments than those in the literature can bring us a better understanding of the points raised" (p. 517).

In rebuttal, Glass and Smith (1978) make several points already mentioned in this chapter and earlier ones. First, as noted in Chapter 2, the poor design characteristics of different studies can "cancel" one another out, if the results of different studies are consistent. Second, the a priori quality judgments required to exclude studies are likely to vary from judge to judge and be influenced by personal biases. Finally, Glass and Smith claim they did not advocate the abandonment of quality standards. Instead, they regarded the impact of design quality on study results as "an empirical a posteriori question, not an a priori matter of opinion" (Glass, McGaw, & Smith, 1981, p. 222). They suggested that reviewers thoroughly code the design aspects, good and bad, of each study and then demonstrate if, in fact, the outcomes of studies are related to how the studies were conducted.

I agree with Glass and his colleagues. The decision to include or exclude studies on an a priori basis requires the reviewer to make an overall judgment of quality that is often too subjective to be credible. Instead, a careful enumeration of study characteristics can be devised by a reviewer and study characteristics can be compared to study results to determine if they covary with one another. If it is empirically demonstrated that studies using "good" methods produce results different from "bad" studies, the results of the good studies can be believed. When no difference is found it is sensible to retain the "bad" studies because they contain other variations in methods (like different samples and locations) that, by their inclusion, will help solve many other questions surrounding the problem area.

The only circumstances in which a priori exclusion of studies may be appropriate are when the criteria for excluding studies are defined before the literature is searched, so that the rules do not shift to suit the reviewer, and the number of acceptable studies is large enough to still permit the reviewer to adequately substantiate any general conclusions that are drawn. In most cases, however, letting the data speak—that is, including all studies and examining empirically the differences in results associated with methods—substitutes a discovery process for the predispositions of the reviewer.

APPROACHES TO CATEGORIZING RESEARCH METHODS

The decision to take an empirical approach to the impact of research methods on research results does not relieve the reviewer of all evaluative responsibilities. The reviewer must still decide what methodological characteristics of studies need to be coded. Obviously these decisions will depend on the nature of the question under scrutiny and the types of associated research. If a problem has been addressed mainly through experimental manipulations in laboratory settings a different set of methodological characteristics may be important than if a correlational, field study, or some mix of the two types of research has been used. In the past, research reviewers have employed two approaches to coding methods so that potential differences between "good" and "bad" studies could be assessed. The first approach requires the reviewer to make judgments about the threats to validity that exist in a study. The second approach requires the detailing of the objective design characteristics of a study, as described by the primary researchers.

The Threats-to-Validity Approach

When Campbell and Stanley (1963) introduced the notion of "threats to validity," they literally transformed the social sciences. They suggested that an identifiable set of extraneous influences associated with each research design could be found which "might produce effects confounded with the experimental stimulus" (p. 5). Different research designs had different validity threats associated with them and designs could be compared according to their inferential capabilities. More importantly, less-than-optimal designs could be "triangulated" so that strong inferences could result from multiple studies when the single, "perfect" study could not be performed.

Campbell and Stanley's notion held the promise of increased sensitivity and objectivity in discussions of research quality. However, it was not long before some problems in the application of Campbell and Stanley's scheme became apparent. The problems related to creating an exhaustive list of threats to validity and identifying what the implication of each threat might be. Initially, Campbell and Stanley (1963) proposed two broad classes of validity threats. Threats to *internal* validity related to the direct correspondence between the experimental treatment and the experimental effect. To the extent that this correspondence was compromised by deficiencies in research design, the interpretability of a study's results would be called into question. Campbell and Stanley listed eight threats to internal validity. Threats to *external* validity related to the generalizability of research results. Evaluating external validity required assessing the representativeness of a study's participants, settings, treatments, and measurement variables. While the external validity of a study could never be assessed definitively, Campbell and Stanley suggested four classes of threats to representativeness.

Next, Bracht and Glass (1968) offered an expanded list of threats to external validity. They felt that "external validity was not treated as comprehensively as internal validity in the Campbell-Stanley chapter" (p. 437). To rectify this omission, Bracht and Glass identified two broad classes of external validity: *population* validity, referring to generalization to persons not included in a study and *ecological* validity referring to nonsampled settings. Two specific threats to population validity were described along with 10 threats to ecological validity.

Later, Campbell (1969) added a ninth threat to internal validity, called "instability," defined as "unreliability of measures, fluctuations in sampling persons or components, autonomous instability of repeated or equivalent measures" (p. 411).

Finally, Cook and Campbell (1979) offered a list of 33 specific threats to validity grouped into four broad classifications. The notions of construct validity and statistical conclusion validity were added to internal and external validity. *Construct* validity referred to "the possibility that the operations which are meant to represent a particular cause or effect construct can be construed in terms of more than one construct" (p. 59). *Statistical conclusion* validity referred to the power and appropriateness of the data analysis technique.

From this brief history, the problems in using the threats-to-validity approach to assess the quality of empirical studies should be clear. First, different researchers may use different lists of threats. For instance, should the threat of "instability" offered by Campbell (1969) constitute one threat, as originally proposed, or three threats, as redefined by Cook and Campbell (1979)? Or should ecological validity constitute one threat or up to 10 different threats? A second problem is the relative weighting of threats—is the threat of "history" weighted equally with the threat of "restricted generalizability across constructs"? Expert methodologists may even disagree on how a particular threat should be classified. For instance, Bracht and Glass (1968) listed "experimenter expectancy effects" as a threat to external validity while Cook and Campbell (1979) listed it as a threat to the construct validity of causes.

All these problems aside, the threats-to-validity approach to the evaluation of research still represents an improvement in rigor, and is certainly preferable to the a priori single judgment of quality it replaces. Each successive list of threats represents an increase in precision and accumulation of knowledge. Also, the list of validity threats gives the reviewer an explicit set of criteria to apply or modify. In that sense, reviewers who use the threats-to-validity approach make their rules of judgment open to criticism and debate. This is a crucial step in making the research evaluation process more objective.

The Methods-Description Approach

In the second approach to study evaluation, the reviewer codes exhaustively the objective characteristics of each study's methods, as they are described by the primary researchers. This approach was discussed earlier in connection with the study coding sheet (see Chapter 2). Now a more detailed examination is in order.

In Campbell and Stanley's (1963) original work, three pre-experimental designs, three true experimental designs, and ten quasi-experimental designs were examined. The list of designs was expanded by Cook and Campbell (1979). In most areas of research considerably fewer than these two dozen or so designs will be needed to describe exhaustively how independent and dependent variables have been paired in the relevant research.

As Campbell and Stanley (1963) noted, experimental designs relate mainly to eliminating threats to internal validity. They hold little information about other threats to trustworthiness. Examining the credibility of, say, experimental manipulations and measurements requires a description of the procedures that the primary researchers used to create independent variables and measure dependent variables. With regard to manipulated independent variables, reviewers can code the number and type of empirical realizations used: In how many ways was the independent variable manipulated? Was the manipulation accomplished through written instructions, films, or the creation of a live-action situation? Similarly reviewers can record the presence or absence of controls to keep the experimenter blind to the treatment conditions and whether deception or misdirection was used to lead the participant away from guessing the hypothesis. Obviously these considerations are relevant only when treatment manipulations were employed in the studies of interest.

Distinctions in measurement techniques can be codified by recording the number of measures used; whether they were verbal, written, behavioral, or interpersonal judgments; whether they were standardized, informal, or constructed for the particular study; and their relative reliability, if such assessments are available. Other measurement characteristics might be of interest to particular research areas.

As to the generalizability of results, the reviewer can record any restrictions on the types of individuals sampled in the primary studies, when and where the studies were conducted, and when the dependent variable measurements were taken in relation to the manipulation or measurement of the independent variables.

To assess a study's statistical analyses, reviewers should record the number of participants, whether a between- or within-subjects design was employed, the number of other factors (sources of variance) extracted by the analyses, and the statistical test used.

One problem with the methods-description approach to evaluation studies is shared with the threats-to-validity approach—different reviewers may choose to list different methodological characteristics. However, the methods-description approach has several advantages. First, when studies are being coded the methods-description approach does not require as much integration of material or inferential judgment. Making a judgment about the threat to validity called "low statistical power" provides a good example. The coder of a study can make this judgment only through a combination of several explicit study characteristics: size of the sample, between- or within-subjects design, inherent power of the statistical test (e.g., parametric vs. nonparametric), and/or number of other sources of variance extracted in the analysis. Two coders of the same study might disagree on whether or not a study is low in power, but perfectly agree on a coding of the separate components that make up the decision. The objective design characteristics of studies can be coded with less ambiguity of meaning and, therefore, greater reliability. The question then becomes: Is the integration of methodological information when studies are first coded necessary to assess the presence or absence of a validity threat? For a majority of threats, the answer is no. If an analysis of study results shows that, say, only studies using within-subjects designs found significant results, then the reviewer can examine this design feature for all of its implications for validity. That is, between-subjects designs may have been too low in power to reveal an effect, or the premeasure in the within-subjects designs may have sensitized the participants to the independent variable manipulation. Thus, while it may be difficult to retrieve the particular aspect of a research design that created a threat to validity, the reviewer often can still examine validity threats when methodological distinctions are coded.

A Mixed-Criteria Approach

The optimal strategy for categorizing studies appears to be a mix of the two a posteriori approaches. First, the reviewer should code all potentially relevant, objective aspects of research design. However, there are threats to validity that may not be captured by this information alone. For instance, the threats to internal validity involving how a control group is treated—i.e., diffusion of treatments, compensatory rivalry, or resentful demoralization in the less desirable treatment—are probably best coded directly as threats to validity, though deciding whether they are present or absent still relies heavily on the description of the study presented by the primary researcher. While this mixed-criteria approach does not remove all problems from study evaluation, it is another step toward explicit objective decision making in an area previously rife with subjective and arbitrary judgments.

The illustrative reviews. Two of the four illustrative reviews provide good examples of how research evaluations can be conducted.

First, studies of the relation between locus of control and achievement included only associational research designs, so the covered studies varied little in internal validity. However, the generalizability of results, trustworthiness of measures, and statistical analyses still needed careful scrutiny for their potential impact on study results.

The coders of individual locus of control and achievement studies made no inferences whatever about methods or their validity—they simply gathered information exactly as reported by the primary researchers. For instance, the participants' gender, age, location, and ethnic and social class backgrounds were all variables that could potentially relate to the external validity or generalizability of results. Using a sample of participants restricted along these lines, however, was not seen as a cause for a priori elimination of the study. Instead, review-generated evidence was used to determine empirically if a sampling restriction affected a result.

In the review of drug treatments of hyperactivity the selection of studies was restricted to include only those that employed random assignment and double blind procedures, the strongest possible design for causal inferences. Thus this review did exclude studies on an a priori basis. What was the rationale? Sixty-one studies were found that met very strict methodological requirements—a majority of all the studies identified as potentially relevant. This was a large enough pool of experiments to examine effectively the impact of other procedures on study results. That is, other aspects of studies related to other forms of validity varied considerably even within this restricted sample. It will be rare for this type of situation to prevail in the social sciences. When it does the reviewer may be able to argue convincingly for a priori exclusion of studies. Certainly it would be difficult for a critic of the hyperactivity review to argue that the exclusion of studies was biased by the reviewers' predispositions.

PROBLEMS IN DATA RETRIEVAL

Thus far procedures have been discussed that allow reviewers to find and evaluate research in an exhaustive and rigorous fashion. Some deficiencies in both retrieval and evaluation procedures have been noted that will frustrate even reviewers with the best of intentions. Some potentially relevant studies do not become public and therefore defy the grasp of even the most conscientious search procedures. With regard to evaluating studies, it is impossible to remove subjectivity from the process completely. A third problem area spans both the retrieval and evaluation phases of literature reviewing. These problems, almost completely beyond the control of the reviewer, involve (1) the inability of libraries to ensure that all documents of potential relevance to the reviewer are on hand, (2) the careless or incomplete reporting of data by primary researchers and (3) the less-than-perfect information processing skills of the people who retrieve information from studies. Each of the three problems will be dealt with separately.

Problems in Library Retrieval

Every research reviewer will find that some articles of potential relevance (based on their title or abstract) cannot be located in their personal or institutional library. To what lengths should the reviewer go to retrieve these articles? The use of interlibrary loans is a viable route for attempting to retrieve these studies. Contacting the primary researchers directly is another possibility, although personal contact often results in only a low rate of response. Whether or not a primary researcher can be located and induced to send a reprint is influenced in part by the age of the article requested.

In general, when deciding how to retrieve articles that are difficult to obtain the searcher should consider (1) the percentage of the total of known articles that are difficult to find, (2) the availability of interlibrary loan procedures, and (3) the likelihood that personal requests to primary researchers will be answered. Factors that might influence each of these considerations are the amount of money available to undertake these retrieval procedures and any time constraints under which the reviewer is operating.

Incomplete and Erroneous Results Sections

Perhaps the most frustrating occurrence in study retrieval is when the reviewer obtains a primary research report but the report is incomplete in its description of the results. For instance, this author's review of research on gender differences in conformity (Cooper, 1979) found that 12 of 38 relevant research reports contained no description of the statistics that led to the conclusion. Statistical data were most often omitted from a report when the results of the tests were nonsignificant. Most remarkable was the discovery of four studies that did report statistical data but neglected to mention the direction of the relation!

Obviously incomplete reporting of statistical values will be of primary concern to research reviewers who intend to perform quantitative synthesis (discussed in the next chapter). What should the quantitative reviewer do about missing data? Several conventions can be suggested to handle the most common problems.

First, the reviewer can treat all studies that report hypothesis tests as "nonsignificant" without reporting the associated F-tests, p-levels, or effect sizes as having uncovered exactly null results. That is, for any statistical analysis involving these studies, a probability of .5 (in the one-tailed instance) and a relationship strength of zero is assumed. It is reasonable to expect that this convention has a conservative impact on any quantitative review results. In general, when this convention is used, cumulative p-levels should be higher and the average relationship strength closer to zero than if the exact results of these studies were known.

Another convention involves attempting to combine results when some primary researchers use parametric statistics and others use nonparametric statistics. In most cases one statistical paradigm will predominate greatly over the other across the entire set of studies. In this instance the different statistics can be aggregated as though they all shared the dominant set of assumptions without greatly distorting the results. If the split between parametric and nonparametric tests is roughly even, the two sets of studies should be examined separately.

Reviewers who want to perform statistical combinations sometimes find separate studies are incommensurable because they employ different numbers of factors in their analysis. For instance, one study on drug treatments of hyperactive children might present a simple t-test comparison of a treated and control group. Another study might have employed the gender and age of children as additional factors in an analysis of variance design. All else being equal—and assuming some gender and age effect—the second experiment will produce a lower probability level and a larger treatment effect because the amount of error against which the treatment-control difference is compared will be smaller. Glass et al. (1981) have outlined procedures for equating statistical results from studies using different numbers of factors in their analytic design. But in practice primary researchers rarely report their results in enough detail to carry out the needed transformations. When this is the case, the reviewer should determine empirically whether the statistical results of a study are related to the number of factors in the analysis. If a relation is found, the reviewer should report separately the results obtained from analyses of studies that used only the single factor of interest. In addition to incomplete reports, some reports are inexact in their statistical data. Many reports will describe statistical tests as reaching the $p <$ .05 level of significance rather than describing the exact probability associated with the outcome of the inference test. In this case the reviewer can recalculate the p-levels to reflect their exact value.

Finally, there is the problem of errors in statistical analyses. As an empirical demonstration, Wolins (1962) contacted 37 psychologists who had recently published research reports and asked if he could see their raw data, and 26, or 70%, did not reply or claimed their data had been lost or inadvertently destroyed. Of 7 data sets Wolins was able to reanalyze, 3 were found to have large analytic errors.

While no one knows exactly how common errors are in statistical analyses, studies indicate they may be frequent enough to concern research reviewers. Whenever possible, the reviewer should cross-check the statistics presented in research reports to ensure that none of the results are or imply wild values and all of the results reported about a study are consistent with one another.

Unreliability in Coding Study Results

Just as researchers sometimes make errors in their data analysis, it is also the case that errors are made in the recording of data. Transcription errors are a problem for research reviewers when they extract information from research reports. Rosenthal (1978a) reviewed 21 studies that examined the frequency and distribution of recording errors. These studies uncovered error rates ranging from 0% to 4.2% of all the data recorded; 64% of the errors in recording were in a direction that tended to confirm the study's initial hypothesis.

Stock and colleagues (1982) empirically examined the number of unreliable codings made in a literature review. They had three coders (one statistician, and two post-Ph.D. educational researchers) record data from 30 documents into 27 different coding categories. Stock and colleagues found that some variables, such as the means and standard deviations of the ages of participants, were coded with perfect or near perfect agreement. Only one judgment, concerning the type of sampling procedure employed by the researchers, did not reach an average coder agreement of 80%.

In sum, while coders of primary research are fairly reliable in their retrieval of information, it is good practice to monitor coder accuracy. This is especially true if the number of studies to be coded is large or if persons with limited research training are called upon to do the coding. In these instances the reviewer should treat the coding of studies as if it were a standard exercise in data gathering. Specifically, coding sheets should be accompanied by codebooks explaining the meaning of each entry. Prior to actual coding, discussions and practice examples should be worked on with coders. Assessments of reliability should be taken on controlled sets of studies. Coding should not begin until an acceptable level of intercoder reliability has been established.

The illustrative reviews. The retrieval and reporting problems discussed above appeared in several of the illustrative reviews. As mentioned earlier, the review of ethnic and social class differences in need for achievement presented the biggest problem with regard to unretrievable research reports. This problem was created mainly by the international nature of the topic—meaning many of the manuscripts or journals containing potentially relevant research were not available in the institutional libraries. Thus the review was restricted explicitly to published studies. Even among published studies, however, the percentage of reports that were available was only 69%. The potential impact of this difficulty on the findings was explicated carefully in the review report.

Incomplete data reporting created the greatest problem for the review of locus of control and achievement. Of 275 hypothesis tests covered in the review, 55 needed to be assigned to an "exact zero" category because the primary researchers reported a nonsignificant effect without accompanying statistics. Furthermore, 23 reports gave a direction for the results of the hypothesis test but neither a statement about the test's significance or its magnitude. Luckily, the direction of findings in these studies was roughly consistent with findings for which full information was given. However, these studies could not be included in the quantitative analyses.

IDENTIFYING INDEPENDENT
HYPOTHESIS TESTS

A final decision that must be made during the data evaluation stage involves determining the number of hypothesis-relevant tests contained in a research report. Sometimes a single research report may contain multiple tests of the same hypothesis. These multiple tests may occur because (1) different samples of people were used in the study and their data were analyzed separately, (2) multiple measures of the same construct were employed in the study and each measure was analyzed separately, or (3) a single paper reports more than one research project. Especially in instances where the reviewer intends to perform a quantitative synthesis, a decision must be made about whether or not each hypothesis test should be considered an independent event. Several strategies can be suggested regarding how to decide on the unit of analysis in research reviews.

Laboratories as Units

The most conservative approach to the identification of independent hypothesis tests employs the laboratory or researcher as the smallest unit of analysis. This approach requires the reviewer to gather all studies done at the same research laboratory and to come to some overall conclusion concerning the results of that particular site. The rationale behind this strategy is that research conducted at the same site, even if it appears in separate reports in different journals over a number of years, still contains certain constancies that imply the results are not completely independent of one' another. The same primary researcher with the same predispositions may be using the same laboratory room and the same research assistants while drawing participants from the same population. In some subject areas, it might not be unusual to find dozens of studies relevant to a single hypothesis being contributed by the same primary researcher. Advocates of this most conservative approach would suggest that the information value of repeated studies in the same laboratory is not as great as an equal number of studies reported from separate laboratories. (An intra-class r can be computed to assess the empirical degree of independence of studies from the same laboratory.) One drawback to this approach is that it requires the reviewer to conduct reviews within reviews, since decisions about how to synthesize results first must be made within laboratories and then again between laboratories.

Studies as Units

Using the study as the unit of analysis requires the reviewer to make an overall decision about the results of comparisons reported in separate journal articles or manuscripts but not to aggregate results over more than one report. If a single research report contains information on more than one test of the same hypothesis, the reviewer using this strategy weights each discrete finding by the number of hypothesis tests in the report or study. This ensures that each study contributes equally to the overall review result. A study with three subsamples of participants reporting results on five different measures of the same variable (e.g., 15 hypothesis tests) might be weighted so that a single result comes from the report and this result is given consideration equal to a report with one sample and one measure.

Obviously there will be some subjectivity in the reviewer's judgment of what constitutes a study. For instance, one reviewer might consider all results in a single report as one study. But another reviewer might consider a report that divides results into separate studies as containing more than one study. Thus the delineation is not clear as in the case of defining laboratories or experimenters.

Statistical Tests as Units

The least conservative approach to identifying comparisons is to use the individual statistical test as the unit of analysis. Each separate test of the hypothesis conducted by primary researchers is regarded as an independent test by the research reviewer. This technique's strength is that it does not lose any of the within-study information regarding potential moderators of the relation. Its weakness is that the assumption that hypothesis tests are independent, needed for most quantitative syntheses of results, will be violated. Also the results of studies will not be weighted equally in any overall conclusion of results. Instead studies will contribute to the overall finding in relation to the number of statistical tests contained in it. This is not necessarily a good weighting criterion.

Shifting Units

A compromise approach to identifying comparisons is to employ a shifting unit of analysis. Specifically, each statistical test is initially coded as if it were an independent event. Thus a single study that contained 12 statistical tests would have 12 separate coding sheets filled out for it. Each coding sheet would be slightly different, depending on the aspects of the samples, measurements, or design characteristics used to distinguish the statistical test. However, when an overall cumulative result for the review is generated, statistical tests are weighted so that each *study* (all other weighting factors being equal) contributes equally to the general finding. Thus a study containing, say, three correlations between locus of control and achievement would have these three correlations averaged and then added as a single number into the analysis across all studies. However, when examining potential moderators of the overall relation, a study's results are aggregated only *within* the separate categories of the influencing variable. For example, if a locus of control and achievement study presented correlations for males and females separately, this study would contribute only one correlation to the overall analysis—the average of the male and female studies— but two correlations to the analysis of the impact of gender on the relation— one for the female group and one for male group. To take the process one step further, if this study reported different correlations for specific and general locus of control tests within each gender (i.e., four correlations in all), the two correlations for different measurements would be averaged within each gender group when the analysis for gender influence was conducted and the two gender group correlations would be averaged when the specificity of measurement moderator was examined. This means that for moderating hypotheses a single study can contribute one test to each of the categories distinguished by the third variable. This strategy is a compromise which allows studies to retain their maximum information value while keeping to a minimum any violation of the assumption of independence of hypothesis tests.

The illustrative reviews. Three of the four illustrative research reviews employed the shifting unit of analysis procedure described above. The only exception was the review of research design effects on response rates to questionnaires. In this analysis, because the raw data from each study could be retrieved and aggregated, the number of participants in a study determined its weighting. In instances where raw data can be retrieved it should be used rather than sample statistics (see the next chapter for details).

VALIDITY ISSUES IN
EVALUATING RESEARCH

The use of any evaluative criteria other than methodological quality introduces a potential threat to the validity of the review outcome. As Mahoney (1977) states, "To the extent that researchers display [confirmatory] bias our adequate understanding of the processes and parameters of human adaptation may be seriously jeopardized" (p. 162). It is safe to assume that evaluative bias has pernicious effects on our understanding.

A second threat to validity occurring during data evaluation involves the unreliability in data introduced by the incomplete reporting of primary researchers. We have seen that many research reports completely omit discussions of hypothesis tests or give only incomplete information on the tests that were mentioned. The greater the percentage of such incomplete reports within a research review the wider are the confidence intervals that must be placed around the review's conclusion.

Finally, a third threat to the validity of a review involves the unreliability in coding of research results. In most instances coding can be done with fairly high reliability, especially if the strategy employed only asks coders to retrieve information directly as presented by the primary researchers, rather than making inferences about research quality or the presence or absence of particular validity threats.

Protecting validity. In the course of this chapter several procedures have been described that are designed to increase the objectivity of research evaluation and related decisions.

1. Reviewers should make every effort to insure that *only* conceptual judgments influence the decision to include or exclude studies from a review.

2. If studies are to be weighted differently, the weighting scheme should be explicit and justifiable. Personal involvement in a study is not a legitimate criteria for giving it added weight.

3. The approach used to categorize study methods should exhaust as many design moderators as possible. The reviewer should detail each design distinction that was related to study results and tell the outcome of the analysis.

4. More than one study coder should be employed and intercoder agreement should be quantified and reported. Also the coding sheets should be filled out by coders who are blind to the results of the study.

5. The reviewer should state explicitly what conventions were used when incomplete or erroneous research reports were encountered.

EXERCISES

1. List a set of criteria that you think distinguish good and bad research. Rank order the criteria with regard to their impact on research quality. Compare your criteria and rankings with those of a classmate. What is similar and different about your lists?

2. With your classmate, agree on a set of criteria and evaluative scales. Also identify a set of ten studies on the same topic. Independently apply the criteria to the ten articles. Compare your ratings. How did they differ and what led to the differences? How might the criteria be revised to minimize differences in future use?

3. Using the same set of studies, and again in conjunction with a classmate, record the following information from each report: (a) sample size; (b) any restrictions on who was sampled; (c) the means of comparison groups (or other data) on the primary variable of interest; (d) whether or not the hypothesis was confirmed; and (e) the type and significance level of the inference test of primary interest. How many values did you agree and disagree on? Which values led to the most disagreement? Why?

5

The Analysis and Interpretation Stage

This chapter presents some statistical methods that can help reviewers summarize research results. Among the techniques discussed are those that generate cumulative probabilities, those that involve the calculation of an effect size, and those that help the reviewer examine the variability of effect sizes across studies. Finally, validity issues arising during data analysis and interpretation are outlined.

Data analysis and interpretation involves the synthesis of the separate data points collected by the inquirer into a unified statement about the research problem. According to Kerlinger (1973):

> *Analysis* means the categorization, ordering, manipulating and summarizing of data to obtain answers to research questions. The purpose of analysis is to reduce data to intelligible and interpretable form. . . . *Interpretation* takes the results of analysis, makes inferences pertinent to the research relations studied, and draws conclusions about these relations (p. 134).

As noted in the introduction, data interpretation requires that decision rules be used to distinguish systematic data patterns from "noise" or chance fluctuation. Although different decision rules can be used, the rules typically involve assumptions about what noise looks like in the target populations (e.g., normally distributed errors).

INTEGRATING TECHNIQUES IN
THE TWO TYPES OF INQUIRY

Just as any scientific inquiry requires the leap from concrete operations to abstract concepts, both primary researchers and research reviewers must leap from samples of data to more general conclusions. Until recently, however, there has been almost no similarity in the analysis and interpretation techniques used by primary researchers and reviewers. Primary researchers have been obligated to present sample statistics and to substantiate any assertions about hypotheses with probability tests. Most frequently, primary researchers have computed means and standard deviations descriptive of their samples, made the assumptions needed for statistical tests (e.g., normal distribution and independence of errors, homogeneity of variance), and reported the probabilities associated with whether potential sources of systematic variance could be distinguished from error.

Statistical aids to primary data interpretation have not gone uncriticized. Some methodologists have argued that significance tests are not very informative since they only tell whether or not the null hypothesis is true (Bakan, 1966; Lykken, 1968; Nunnally, 1960). They argue that in a population of people the null hypothesis is almost never true and therefore the significance of a given test is mainly influenced by how many participants have been included in the study. Also those skeptical about the value of significance test statistics point to limitations in the population of events referred to under parametric assumptions (Cornfield & Tukey, 1956; Edgington, 1967). No matter how statistically significant a relation may be, the results of a study are only generalizable to people like those who participated in that particular research effort.

Skepticism about the value of statistics helps those who use statistics to refine their skills and keep their output in proper perspective. Nonetheless most primary researchers use statistics in their work and most would feel extremely uncomfortable about synthesizing data without some assistance (or credibility) supplied by statistical procedures.

In contrast to primary researchers, research reviewers have not been obligated to apply any standard analysis and interpretation techniques in the synthesis process. Most frequently reviewers interpret data using rules of inference unknown even to them. Therefore a description of the common rules of inference used in traditional research reviews is not possible. Analysis and interpretation methods have been idiosyncratic to the particular perspective of the individual reviewer. This subjectivity in analysis and interpretation has led many to voice skepticism about the conclusions of many reviews. To address the problem, these critics have introduced quantitative methods into the reviewing process. The methods build on the primary research statistics contained in the individual studies.

THE QUANTITATIVE REVOLUTION

It was suggested above that the two recent events which have had the strongest impact on research reviewing were the growth in research and the advent of the computerized literature search. The third strongest impact is the introduction of quantitative procedures into the reviewing process.

The explosion in social science research has focused considerable attention on the lack of standardization in how reviewers arrive at general conclusions from series of related studies. For some topic areas a separate verbal description of each relevant study will now be impossible. One traditional strategy, to focus on one or two studies chosen from dozens or hundreds, fails to portray accurately the accumulated state of knowledge.

Most certainly, in areas where hundreds of studies exist, reviewers must describe "prototype" studies so that readers understand the methods primary researchers have used. However relying on the *results* of prototype studies as representative of all studies may be seriously misleading. As we have seen, this type of selective attention is open to confirmatory bias: A particular reviewer may highlight only studies which support his or her initial position. Also selectively attending to evidence cannot give a good estimate of the strength of a relation. As evidence on a topic accumulates, researchers become more interested in the strength rather than the simple existence of a relation. Finally, selective attention to only a portion of all studies places little or imprecise weight on the volume of available testings. Presenting one or two studies without a cumulative analysis of the entire set of results gives the reader no estimate of the confidence that should be placed in a conclusion.

Reviewers also face problems when they consider the variation between the results of different studies. Reviewers will find distributions of results for studies sharing a particular procedural characteristic but varying on many other characteristics. They may not be able to conclude accurately whether a procedural variation affects study results because of the variability in results obtained by any single method or the likelihood that the distributions of results with different methods will overlap. It seems, then, that there are many situations in which reviewers must turn to quantitative reviewing techniques. Gene Glass (1977) has written, "The accumulated findings of . . . studies should be regarded as complex data points, no more comprehensible without statistical analysis than hundreds of data points in a single study" (p. 352).

The application of quantitative inference procedures to reviewing seems to be a necessary response to the expanding literature. If statistics are applied appropriately they should enhance the validity of review conclusions. Quantitative reviewing is an extension of the same rules of inference required for rigorous synthesis in primary research. If primary researchers must specify quantitatively the relation of the data to their conclusions, the next users of the data should be required to do the same. The bulk of this chapter will address what quantitative reviewing procedures are available and how they are applied.

When Not to Use Statistics

The value of quantitative reviewing has been questioned along lines similar to criticisms of primary data analysis (e.g., Eysenck, 1978; Mansfield & Bussey, 1977; Barber, 1978). However this author finds that most arguments against quantitative reviewing are spurious. This book, it is hoped, will help to separate the issue of quantitative analysis in reviews from less appropriate reviewing procedures (such as lack of operational detail) which have erroneously been linked to this issue (see Cooper & Arkin, 1981). It is important, however, to state explicitly some circumstances in which the use of quantitative procedures in reviews is *not* needed.

First, the basic premise behind the use of statistics in reviews is that *a series of studies have been identified that address an identical conceptual hypothesis.* If the premises of a review do not include this assertion, then there is no need for cumulative statistics. Quantitative procedures are only applicable to integrative research reviews, not to theoretical or methodological reviews (see Chapter 1). For instance, if a reviewer is interested in tracing the historical development of the concept of hyperactivity, it would not be necessary to do a quantitative review. However, if the review also intended to make an inference about whether different definitions of hyperactivity (i.e., methods for diagnosing it) led to different effectiveness for drug treatment, then a quantitative summary of relevant research would be appropriate.

The drug treatment of hyperactivity illustrative review points out a second limitation on quantitative syntheses. In this review, separate analyses were conducted on comparisons of drug treatments versus placebo control groups and drug treatment versus no treatment control groups. Even though both comparisons assessed the effectiveness of drugs, it would not necessarily be informative to lump them together. When a hypothesis involves a comparison with controls, the reviewer might find that a distinction in the type of control is important enough not to be obscured in a quantitative analysis.

Third, a reviewer should not quantitatively combine studies at a broader conceptual level than readers would find useful. At an extreme, most social science research could be categorized as examining a single conceptual hypothesis—social stimuli affect human behavior. Indeed, for some purposes, such a hypothesis test might be very enlightening. However this should not be used as an excuse to lump together concepts and hypotheses without attention to those distinctions that will be meaningful to the users of the review (see Kazdin, Durac, & Agteros, 1979, for a humorous treatment of this issue). For instance the review on ethnic and social class differences in need for achievement provides an example of when a quantitative combination of studies was possible but not profitable. Forty-two separate comparisons were located which all tested the relation of ethnic origin to achievement strivings. Yet rather than lump them together, the highest level of conceptualization was the ethnic group itself, for example, blacks versus whites, whites versus Mexican-Americans, Australians versus New Zealanders, and so on. To have accumulated results at any broader conceptual level probably would have been of little interest to the review's readers and misleading, since one comparison, black versus white Americans, would have contributed disproportionately to the overall result. It accounted for nearly 25% of all ethnicity comparisons.

Integrating Techniques and Differences in Review Outcomes

While the relative validity of different inference strategies is difficult to assess, Cooper and Rosenthal (1980) did demonstrate some of the objective differences between quantitative and nonquantitative procedures in research reviews. Graduate students and faculty were asked to evaluate a literature on a simple hypothesis—is gender related to task persistence? All reviewers evaluated the same set of studies but half the reviewers used quantitative procedures and half used whatever criteria appealed to them. No reviewer in the latter condition chose quantitative techniques. Statistical reviewers reported more support for the hypothesis and a larger relationship between variables than did nonstatistical reviewers. Statistical reviewers also tended to view future replicative research as less necessary than nonstatistical reviewers, although this finding did not reach statistical significance.

It is also likely that the different statistical tests employed by reviewers who adopt quantitative procedures will create variance in review conclusions. Several different paradigms have emerged for quantitatively reviewing social science research with a parametric model (Glass et al., 1981; Rosenthal & Rubin, 1978; Gage, 1978; Hedges, 1982a), and other paradigms can be used with a Bayesian perspective (Hunter & Schmidt, 1978; Viana, 1980). There are numerous techniques available for combining the separate study probabilities to generate an overall probability for the run of studies (Rosenthal, 1978b, 1980). The different techniques generate probability levels that vary somewhat. Thus the rules adopted to carry out quantitative analysis can differ from reviewer to reviewer and this may create variance in how review results are interpreted. We can assume as well that the rules used by nonquantitative reviewers also vary but their inexplicit nature makes them difficult to compare formally.

SYNTHESIZING MAIN EFFECTS AND INTERACTIONS

Before examining several of the quantitative techniques available to reviewers, it is important to take a closer look at some of the distinct features of accumulated tests of hypotheses. In the chapter on problem formulation, it was pointed out that at first most research reviews focus on tests of main effects. This is primarily because conceptually identical tests of main effects have occurred more frequently than tests of three or more interacting variables. Of course, once the reviewer has discerned whether or not a main effect is present, he or she next turns to potential moderators of the relation or to interaction hypotheses.

In research reviews the principal feature of both main effect and interaction tests is that the significance levels and relationship strengths associated with separate tests of the same hypothesis will vary from one testing to the next and this variability is sometimes dramatic.

Variability in Main Effect Tests

Varying results for tests of main effects can be produced because of two classes of reasons. Perhaps the simplest cause is the one most often overlooked—sampling error. Taveggia (1974) made the point well:

> A methodological principle overlooked by writers of . . . reviews is that research results are *probabilistic*. What this principle suggests is that, in and of themselves, the findings of any single research are meaningless—they may have occurred simply by chance. It also follows that if a large enough number of researches has been done on a particular topic, chance alone dictates that studies will exist that report inconsistent and contradictory findings! Thus, what appears to be contradictory may simply be the positive and negative details of a distribution of findings (pp. 397-398).

Taveggia highlights one of the implications of using probability theory and sampling techniques to make inferences about populations. As an example, suppose it was possible to measure the achievement motivation of every American, black and white. Also, suppose that if such a task were undertaken, it would be found that the two groups' achievement strivings were exactly equal—that is, exactly equal group means existed for the two populations. Still, if 1,000 samples of 50 blacks and 50 whites were taken and the sample means were compared using the $p < .05$ significance level (two-tailed), about 25 comparisons would show a significant difference favoring whites while about 25 favored blacks. This variation in results is an unavoidable consequence of the fact that the means estimated by the samples will vary somewhat from the true population values. Therefore just by chance some comparisons will pair black and white sample estimates that vary from their true population values by large amounts and in opposite directions.

In the example given, it is unlikely that the reviewer would be fooled into thinking anything but chance caused the result—after all, 950 comparisons would reveal null effects and significant results would be distributed equally for both possible outcomes. In practical applications, however, the pattern of results is rarely this clear: First, as was pointed out in the chapter on study retrieval, the reviewer might not be aware of all null findings because they are hard to find. Also, even if an overall relation does exist between two variables (that is, the null hypothesis is false), some studies can still show significant results in a direction opposite to the overall conclusion. To continue the example, if the average achievement striving of whites is greater than blacks, it is still possible that some samplings will favor blacks, depending on the size of the relation and the number of comparisons performed. In sum, one source of variance in the results of studies can be chance fluctuations due to the inexactness of sampled estimates.

A second source of variance in main effects is typically of more interest to reviewers: the differences in results created by variations in how studies are conducted and/or who participates in them. For instance, it might be that in the entire population, the difference between white and black achievement strivings is greater in children than adults. In Chapter 2, the notion of review-generated evidence for relations was introduced to describe the procedure of examining how study characteristics associate with variation in study results.

The fact that these two sources of variance in research results exist raises an interesting dilemma for the reviewer. When so-called contradictory findings occur, should the reviewer seek an explanation for them by attempting to identify differences between the methods used in contradicting and supporting studies? Or should the reviewer simply write off the contradictory findings as produced by chance variations due to sampling error? Some tests have been devised to help reviewers answer this question. In effect these tests use "sampling error" as the null hypothesis. If the variation in results across studies is too great to be explained by sampling error, then the reviewer knows to seek explanations elsewhere, that is, in methodological differences between studies. For now, however, it should simply be noted that these two distinct sources of variance in study results need to be considered by reviewers.

Variability in Interaction Tests

Obviously, the factors that create variability in main effects can also affect variability in tests of interaction. Interaction effects are as susceptible to sampling error and procedural variation as main effects. However examining interactions in research reviews presents some unique problems. For ease of presentation, these will be discussed in regard to tests of two-way interactions but the remarks generalize to higher order interactions as well.

Figure 5.1 illustrates the results of two hypothetical studies demonstrating interactions. In Study I, the hyperactivity levels of two samples of children are examined. Drug intervention and control conditions are compared on the first day and the seventh day of treatment. On Day 1 children receiving drug treatment are less hyperactive than control children but on Day 7 those children receiving drug treatment are considerably more hyperactive than those not receiving drug treatment. Thus the effect of the drug treatment on hyperactivity reverses itself over the course of the study.

In hypothetical Study II, on Day 1 children receiving the drug treatment are less hyperactive than children in the control group but on Day 5 no difference between the drug and control group is found. Here the effect of the drug treatment "disappears" between the first and second measurement of hyperactivity.

A reviewer uncovering two studies with these findings might be tempted at first glance to conclude that they produced inconsistent results. Study I indicates that drug treatments are initially effective but with the passage of time they actually become counterproductive. Study II evidences no counter-

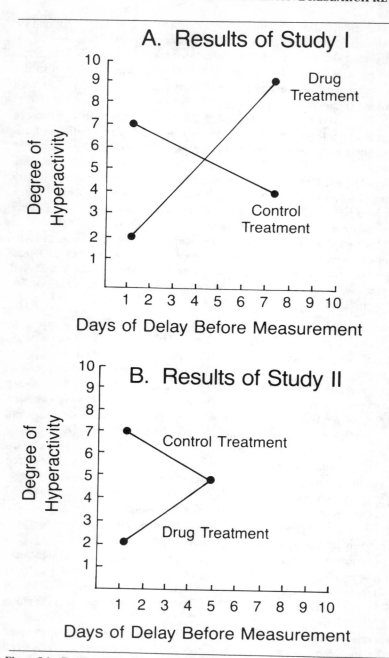

Figure 5.1: Results of Two Hypothetical Studies of Drug Treatment of Hyperactivity

productive effect, just a vanishing of the desired result. A closer examination of the two figures, however, illustrates why it might not be appropriate to conclude that the studies are inconsistent. The results of Study II probably would have been closely approximated by the researchers in Study I if they had taken a measurement of hyperactivity on Day 5. Likewise, had Study II contained a Day 7 measurement, these researchers probably would have produced results quite similar to the Day 7 results contained in Study I. In general researchers who find the experimental effect appears at only one level of an interacting variable can only speculate about whether sampling from more extended levels of that variable would have led to a criss-crossing of the effects. Research reviewers, however, may have an opportunity to draw such conclusions more confidently.

As the example demonstrates, the research reviewer must not assume that different forms or strength of interactions uncovered by different studies necessarily imply an inconsistency of results. Instead research reviewers need to examine the differing levels of variables employed in different studies and if possible to chart results taking the different variable levels into account. In this manner one of the benefits of research reviewing is realized. While one study suggests that the effect of a drug on hyperactivity dissipates over time and another study suggests that the drug effect reverses itself over time, the research reviewer can find that the two results are in fact perfectly commensurate.

This possibility also underscores the importance of primary researchers presenting detailed information concerning the levels of variables used in their studies. Without specific information research reviewers may not be able to conduct an across-study analysis similar to the one presented above. If the primary researchers in Study I and Study II neglected to specify how long a delay was used between measurements, perhaps referring to the two measurement intervals as, say, "short" and "long," the commensurability of the results would have been impossible to demonstrate.

Research reviewers must also carefully examine the statistical analyses that accompany reports of interactions. For instance, all else being equal, it is more likely that the researchers of Study I reported a significant interaction between time of measurement and treatment than did the researchers in Study II. In fact, assuming equal error terms, the F-value in Study I for the interaction should be several times greater than that in Study II.

In sum, it is extremely important that reviewers retrieve the most detailed data about interactions regardless of statistical significance. The problem, of course, is that unless the interaction was the chief concern of the primary researchers or unless the interaction proved significant, there is little likelihood that information detailed enough to perform the kind of analysis portrayed in Figure 5.1 will be contained in the report.

Interactions in Quantitative Reviews

The statistical combination of interactions in quantitative reviews is a very complex task. In fact reviews rarely combine the statistical results of studies examining the same interaction (see Zuckerman, DePaulo, & Rosenthal, 1981, for an example). This may be partly due to the infrequency with which studies have tested the same interaction and partly to the incomplete reporting of many tests of interaction.

There are two different ways that interactions could be statistically combined across studies. First, the separate p-levels and relationship strengths associated with each study's interaction test could be aggregated. An alternative strategy would be to aggregate separately the relation of two variables at each level of the third variable. For instance a hyperactivity review could generate an estimate of the treatment effect by aggregating all measures taken with a one-day delay and compare this to an aggregation of all measures taken with a seven-day delay. This would probably be more useful and easily interpretable to readers than a direct estimate of the magnitude of the interaction effect. However it is rare for primary research reports to contain the information needed to isolate the different simple main effects.

TECHNIQUES FOR COMBINING
PROBABILITIES OF INDEPENDENT STUDIES

In this section and several that follow, brief introductions to some of the quantitative techniques that are available to reviewers will be presented. The techniques were chosen because of their simplicity and broad applicability. The treatment of each technique will be conceptual and introductory. The reader who wants a fuller description of the techniques covered as well as many techniques not mentioned is advised to consult the primary sources cited in the text. In particular, the reader might consult Robert Rosenthal's complementary text in this series (Rosenthal, 1984). For the discussion that follows I assume the reader has a working knowledge of the basic statistical concepts and methods employed in the social sciences.

A major reason why statistical techniques are used in research reviews is to combine the probability levels associated with separate comparisons to generate an overall probability relating to the existence of a relation. For instance if three tests of a relation find statistically significant results and seven find null results, what is the reviewer to conclude? The techniques for combining probabilities allow the reviewer to synthesize the results of numerous tests so that overall conclusions can be drawn.

Three assumptions are crucial to the validity of a conclusion based on a cumulation of individual comparisons. First and most obviously, the individual comparisons that go into a cumulative analysis should all test the same conceptual hypothesis. Regardless of how conceptually broad or narrow the idea might be, the reviewer should be comfortable with the assertion that all the included comparisons address the same question.

Second, the separate comparisons that go into the cumulative analysis must be independent of one another. Identifying independent comparisons was discussed in the chapter on data evaluation. The quantitative reviewer must take care to identify comparisons so that it can be argued that each one contains unique information about the hypothesis.

Finally, the reviewer must believe that the assumptions made by the primary researchers to compute initially the results of the comparison were valid. Thus if the reviewer wishes to combine the probabilities associated with a series of t-test comparisons, the reviewer must assume that the observations, residuals, or errors of the two groups are independent and normally distributed and that the variances are roughly equal.

Vote Counting Methods

The simplest methods for combining results of independent comparisons are the vote counting methods. Vote counts can be done on the direction of the results of comparisons or on the frequency of statistically significant findings.

To do a vote count of directional results, the reviewer must first count the number of comparisons that report results in one direction (called positive, for presentation purposes) and compare this to the number of comparisons reporting results in the other direction (called negative). In this analysis the reviewer ignores the statistical significance of the separate findings. Once the number of results in each direction are counted, the reviewer performs a sign test to discover if the cumulative results suggest one direction occurs more frequently than chance would suggest. If the null hypothesis is true—that is, if no relation between the variables under consideration exists in the population—we would expect the number of findings in each direction to be equal. The formula for computing the sign test is as follows:

$$Z_{vc} = \frac{(N_p) - (\frac{1}{2} \times N_t)}{\frac{1}{2}\sqrt{N_t}} \quad [1]$$

where

Z_{vc} = the standard normal deviate, or Z-score, for the overall series of comparisons;

N_p = the number of positive findings; and

N_t = the total number of comparisons (positive plus negative findings).

The Z_{vc} can be referred to a table of standard normal deviates to discover the probability (one-tailed) associated with the cumulative set of directional findings. If a two-tailed p-level is desired, the tabled value should be doubled.

For example, if 25 of 36 comparisons find results in the positive direction, the probability that the positive and negative directions have an equal chance to occur in the population is $p < .02$ (two-tailed; Z_{vc} equals 2.33). Therefore this result would lead the reviewer to conclude a positive relation was supported by the series of studies.

A practical problem with the directional vote count is that primary researchers frequently do not report the direction of results, especially if a comparison proved statistically nonsignificant. An alternative vote counting method is to perform a sign test on the frequency of only statistically significant results reported in the positive direction versus the frequency of significant results reported in the negative direction. In performing this procedure, the reviewer assumes that under the null hypothesis of no relation in the population, the frequency of significant positive and negative results (in the null case, Type I errors) are expected to be equal (Hedges & Olkin, 1980). The reviewer should bear in mind, however, that the number of nonsignificant findings under the null assumption is expected to be much greater than the number of either positive or negative significant findings. Therefore it is *not* legitimate to test for equal frequencies across the three classes of outcomes (positive, negative, and nonsignificant findings). Hedges and Olkin (1980) have shown that if a reviewer makes the assumption that when no relation exists in the population the number of positive, negative, *and* null findings will be equal, then the vote count method is extremely conservative (that is, likely to miss relations that exist). For instance, assume that a correlation of $r = +.30$ exists between two variables in a population and 20 comparisons have been conducted with 40 people in each comparison. The chance that the vote count associated with this series of studies will be significant if the assumption of equal numbers of each finding is used is only $p = .059$!

Adjusting the expected frequencies of the three findings so that the disproportionate number of expected nonsignificant findings is taken into account solves the theoretical problem but raises a practical one. We have seen that null results are less likely to be reported by researchers and thus are less likely to be retrieved by reviewers. Therefore, if the appropriate theoretical values are used in a vote count analysis, it should often occur that both positive and negative results appear *more* frequently than expected. It seems therefore that using the frequency of nonsignificant findings in a vote count procedure is of dubious value.

In sum, then, a reviewer can perform vote counts to aggregate results across individual studies by comparing the number of "raw" directional findings or of significant findings in the two directions. Both of these procedures will be conservative (i.e., will miss relations that exist) because much information will be lost—the raw direction of results will not appear in many research reports in one case and nonsignificant findings cannot contribute to the analysis in the other case. Vote counting methods should be used only when the number of studies to be aggregated is large and should be supplemented with more sensitive procedures.

Combining Significance Tests

Rosenthal (1978b) cataloged seven different methods for cumulating results that use as their basic data the precise probability values associated with each comparison. The simplest and most routinely applicable of the seven methods will be presented here. The method, called Adding Zs by Rosenthal, was first introduced by Stouffer in 1949.

The Adding Zs method uses the following formula:

$$Z_{st} = \frac{\sum_{i=1}^{N} Z_i}{\sqrt{N}} \qquad [2]$$

where

Z_{st} = the standard normal deviate, or Z-score, for the overall series of comparisons;

Z_i = the standard normal deviate for the ith comparison; and

N = the total number of comparisons in the series.

The steps to carry out the analysis are simple. The reviewer must:

(1) choose which direction for the hypothesis will be considered positive and which negative;
(2) record the probability associated with each comparison;
(3) if the reported probability is two-tailed, halve it;
(4) look up the Z-score associated with each probability;
(5) sum the Z-scores, remembering to place a minus sign before negative results; and
(6) divide this sum by the square root of the number of comparisons.

The resulting Z_{st} can then be referred to a table of standard normal deviates to discover the probability associated with the cumulative set of individual probabilities. If a two-tailed probability is desired, the tabled p-level should be doubled. The probability describes the combined likelihood that the series of results included in the analysis could have been generated by chance if the null hypothesis were true for every study.

Table 5.1 presents a hypothetical application of the Adding Zs method. Note that hypothetical Studies 2 and 7 produced exact null results (probably due to inexact reporting). Studies 1 and 5 produced statistically significant results, and Study 4 produced a result opposite to that predicted.

The method of Adding Zs can be modified to allow the reviewer to differentially weight the results of different comparisons (see Mosteller & Bush, 1954, or Rosenthal, 1978b). For instance, if several comparisons come from a single study, the reviewer might want to weight these less than another comparison which is the only contribution of another study. Or, the reviewer might want to give added weight to studies based on larger sample sizes.

The formula for the Adding Weighted Zs method is:

$$Z_w = \frac{\sum_{i=1}^{N} W_i Z_i}{\sqrt{\sum_{i=1}^{N} W_i^2}} \qquad [3]$$

where

Z_w = the Z-score for the weighted combination of studies;
W_i = the weighting factor associated with each study; and
      all other terms are defined as before.

Table 5.1 presents a hypothetical example of the Adding Weighted Zs method, with the weighting factor being the sample size of the study.

The Fail-safe N

It has been mentioned several times that not all comparisons have an equal likelihood of being retrieved by the reviewer. Nonsignificant results are less likely to be retrieved than significant ones. This fact implies that the Adding Zs method may produce a probability level (chance of a Type 1 error) that is an underestimate. Rosenthal (1979a) wrote, "The extreme view of this problem . . . is that the journals are filled with the 5% of studies that show Type 1 errors, while the file drawers back in the lab are filled with the 95% of studies that show insignificant (e.g., $p > .05$) results" (p. 638). The problem is probably not this dramatic but it does exist.

One of the advantages of the Adding Zs method is that it allows the calculation of a Fail-safe N (see Cooper, 1979 or Rosenthal, 1979a). The Fail-safe N answers the question, "How many comparisons totalling to a null hypothesis confirmation (e.g., $Z_{st} = 0$) would have to be added to the results of the retrieved comparisons in order to change the conclusion that a relation exists?" Rosenthal (1979a) called this the "tolerance for future null results." The formula for calculating this number, when the chosen significance level is $p < .05$ is:

$$N_{FS.05} = \left(\frac{\sum_{i=1}^{N} Z_i}{1.645} \right)^2 - N \qquad [4]$$

TABLE 5.1
A Hypothetical Example of the Combination of Eight Comparisons

Study	Number of Participants	One-Tailed p-Level	Associated Z-Score
1	48	.025	1.96
2	28	.50	0
3	32	.33	.44
4	24	.90	−1.28
5	64	.01	2.33
6	40	.39	.28
7	20	.50	0
8	30	.15	1.04

Adding Zs: $Z_{st} = \dfrac{4.77}{\sqrt{8}} = 1.69$, p < .0461, one-tailed

Adding Weighted Zs: $Z_w = \dfrac{268.96}{\sqrt{11684}} = 2.49$, p < .0064, one-tailed

$N_{FS.05} = \left(\dfrac{4.77}{1.645}\right)^2 -8 = .41$ (or 1)

NOTE: The one-tailed p-level of .90 is from a study finding a direction opposite to that predicted (thus the associated Z-score is negative).

where

$N_{FS.05}$ = the number of additional null-summing comparisons needed to raise the combined probability to just above p < .05;

1.645 = the standard normal deviate associated with p < .05 (one-tailed); and

all other quantities are defined as before.

Obviously, the Fail-safe N cannot be computed when studies are weighted unequally, unless the reviewer wishes to estimate what the average weight of unretrieved comparisons might be—a dubious estimate at best. A hypothetical example of a Fail-safe N is presented in Table 5.1.

The Fail-safe N is a valuable descriptive statistic. It allows the users of a review to evaluate the cumulative result of the review against their assessment of how exhaustively the reviewer has searched the literature. However, the Fail-safe N also contains an assumption which restricts its validity. That is, its user must find credible the proposition that the sum of the unretrieved studies is equal to an exact null result. It might be the case that unretrieved studies have a cumulative result opposite to that contained in the review—perhaps because primary researchers did not want to publish studies that contradicted studies already in print. Or unretrieved studies might cumulatively add support to the conclusion because the reviewer ignored information channels that paralleled those that were used. The plausibility of these alternatives should always be assessed when a Fail-safe N is interpreted.

When is a Fail-safe N large enough so that reviewers and readers can conclude a finding is resistant to unretrieved null results? Rosenthal (1979b) suggested the resistance number equal 5 times the number of retrieved studies plus 10. No steadfast rule is intuitively obvious, so reviewers should argue anew for the resistance of their findings each time the formula is applied. The best argument for a resistant finding is a large Fail-safe N coupled with a comprehensive search strategy.

Combining Raw Data

The most desirable technique for combining results of independent studies is to integrate the raw data from each relevant comparison. The separate data points can be placed into an analysis of variance or multiple regression that employs the comparison that generated the data as a blocking variable. Obviously instances in which the integration of raw data can be achieved are rare. Raw data are seldom included in research reports and attempts to obtain raw data from researchers often end in failure (see Chapter 4).

The benefits of integrating raw data can also be achieved, however, if the reviewer has access to the means and standard deviations associated with each comparison. A problem with the use of means and standard deviations is that the dependent variable measurements in the separate comparisons are often not commensurate with one another—that is, they use different scales with different values. Of course, the reviewer can standardize the measurements in each comparison to make them commensurate. Again, however, the reporting of individual group means and standard deviations in primary research reports is infrequent, though certainly not as rare as the reporting of raw data.

In sum, analyzing raw data from separate comparisons is the optimum strategy for accumulating results. It is the level of analysis to which the reviewer should aspire and its feasibility should be assessed before other less adequate means for combining results are undertaken. In practice, however, the use of this technique is rare.

Combined Results and Study-Generated Evidence

In Chapter 2 the distinction between study-generated and review-generated evidence was discussed. It was pointed out that study-generated evidence is present when a single study contains results that directly test the relation being considered. The results of the cumulative analyses techniques presented thus far produce study-generated evidence. That is, each individual comparison being integrated has something to say about the hypothesis under consideration. Therefore if the individual comparisons have used random assignment of participants to conditions in order to uncover causal mechanisms, the combined results of these comparisons relate to these causal mechanisms. Based on vote counts or combined probabilities, the reviewer can make assertions about causality if in fact the primary research included experimental manipulations. A similar assertion cannot be made about the evidence generated by an examination of research methods that covary with results, a topic to be pursued shortly.

The illustrative reviews. In the review of the relationship between locus of control and achievement, 275 hypothesis tests were uncovered. Of these, 193 resulted in a positive relation, 25 resulted in a negative relation, and 55 fell into the null category (two tests of the comparison were reported as significant but the direction of their results was not given). The sign test associated with the 218 directional results was $Z_{vc} = 11.31$. A Z-score this large occurs when the null hypothesis is true less than once in one million times. Therefore it can be concluded that in general more internal locus of control beliefs were associated with higher academic achievement.

The Adding Zs method used a weighting of comparisons so that each separate study contributed equally to the overall finding. Specifically, the 275 comparisons were contained in 98 different study reports. Of these, 75 reports contained either a significant relation and the accompanying statistics or a null relation. In 23 reports, relations were reported without statistics. These were not included in the analyses, making them somewhat conservative (because the excluded studies favored the positive direction). The weighted Z_{st} covering the 75 studies was 11.08. Again, the probability that this result for a run of studies could be associated with a null relation in the population is far less than one in a million. The Fail-safe N, the number of null-summing comparisons needed to raise this probability to above $p < .05$, was 3,327. This number is well above Rosenthal's (1979b) conservative suggestion concerning how resistant a result should be to unretrieved null effects (i.e., 385). The cumulative results clearly indicated a positive relation between internality of control beliefs and academic achievement.

The review of research design effects on response rates to questionnaires presented a rare opportunity to combine raw data. Each of the 93 relevant studies reported their raw data. In this case, the raw data was the number of persons contacted and the number who responded. In addition, in all studies the dependent variable, nonresponse, was identical. For instance, 8,577 people participated in studies that experimentally manipulated whether or not a monetary incentive was offered for responding to the questionnaire. Of these, 55.5% of participants who were offered a monetary incentive returned the questionnaire while 35.2% of participants not offered an incentive returned the questionnaire. The chi-square value associated with these figures is 188.1, a highly significant value. The proportions used in these analyses were weighted by the number of persons contacted in each study. Thus those studies with larger samples contributed more to this overall result than studies that contained small samples.

MEASURING RELATIONSHIP STRENGTH

The primary function of the statistical procedures described above is to help the reviewer accept or reject the null hypothesis. The null hypothesis, of course, tests the "no relation" hypothesis against all others. Most primary researchers have been content to simply identify hypotheses with some explanatory value—that is, to reject the null. The prevalence of this yes-or-no question is partly due to the relatively recent development of the social sciences. Social hypotheses are crudely stated first approximations to the truth. How potent variables are for explaining human behavior and how competing explanations compare with regard to relative potency are questions which have rarely been asked. As theoretical sophistication has increased, however, more social scientists are making inquiries about the size of relations.

Giving further impetus to the "How much?" question is a growing disenchantment with the null hypothesis significance test itself. Whether or not a null hypothesis can be rejected is tied closely to the particular research project under scrutiny. As mentioned earlier, if an ample number of participants are available or if a sensitive research design is employed, a rejection of the null hypothesis is not surprising. In research reviews this fact becomes even more apparent. An examination of the probabilities associated with the null hypothesis tests in the illustrative reviews makes the point dramatically.

A null hypothesis rejection, then, does not guarantee that an important social insight has been achieved. This point was made by David Lykken (1968): "Statistical significance is perhaps the least important attribute of a good experiment. It is never a sufficient condition for claiming that a theory has been usefully corroborated, that a meaningful empirical fact has been established, or that an experimental report ought to be published" (p. 151). Answering the question "How much?" allows a considerably more informed judgment about explanatory value than does answering the question, "Is it different from zero?"

A Definition of Effect Size

In order to answer meaningfully the "How much?" question, a definition for the notion of relationship strength, or what is more often called the effect size (ES) must be agreed upon. Also we need methods for quantitatively expressing the magnitude of a relation. Jacob Cohen in *Statistical Power Analysis for the Behavioral Sciences* (1977) presented the most thorough and useful examination of the definition of effect sizes. He defines an effect size as follows:

> Without intending any necessary implication of causality, it is convenient to use the phrase "effect size" to mean "the *degree* to which the phenomenon is present in the population," or "the degree to which the null hypothesis is false." By the

above route it can now readily be clear that when the null hypothesis is false, it is false to some specific degree, i.e., *the effect size (ES) is some specific non-zero value in the population.* The larger this value, the greater the *degree* to which the phenomenon under study is manifested (pp. 9-10).

Figure 5.2 presents three hypothetical relationships that illustrate Cohen's definition. Suppose the illustrated results come from three experiments comparing a drug treatment of hyperactivity with a placebo. Figure 5.2A presents a null relationship. That is, the sampled children given the drug have a mean and distribution of hyperactivity scores identical to the placebo-treated children. In Figure 5.2B the treated children have a mean slightly higher than that of the placebo children, and in Figure 5.2C, the difference between treatments is even greater. A measure of effect size must express the three results so that greater departures from the null are associated with higher effect size values.

Cohen's book contains many different metrics for describing the strength of a relation. Each effect size index is associated with a particular research design in a manner similar to t-tests being associated with two-group comparisons, F-tests associated with multi-group designs, and chi-squares associated with frequency tables. The two primary metrics and one secondary metric for describing relationship strength will be presented below. These metrics are generally useful—almost any research outcome can be expressed using one of them. For more detailed information on these effect size metrics, as well as many others, the reader should consult Cohen's (1977) book. However, it is strongly advised that both primary researchers and research reviewers not use effect estimates for multiple degree of freedom tests, even though Cohen lists several of them. All effect sizes should be expressed as comparisons between two groups, as measures of correlation between two continuous variables, or as other single degree of freedom contrasts. The reasoning behind this qualification is simple. In an analysis of variance a multiple degree of freedom F-test tells whether there is significant variability in the array of group means, but it does not tell which groups vary significantly from one another. Therefore in all instances it is essential that multiple degree of freedom significance tests be followed by single degree of freedom comparisons. The same would be true for the effect sizes associated with these tests. If the primary researcher or research reviewer define the problem precisely, he or she should be able to identify single degree of freedom inference tests and associated effect sizes for each comparison of interest. Thus the following discussion is restricted to metrics commensurate with single degree of freedom tests.

The d-Index

The d-index of an effect size is appropriate when the means of two groups are being compared. Thus the d-index is typically used in associa-

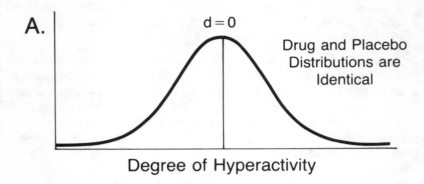

A.

d = 0

Drug and Placebo
Distributions are
Identical

Degree of Hyperactivity

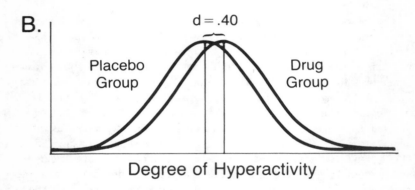

B.

d = .40

Placebo
Group

Drug
Group

Degree of Hyperactivity

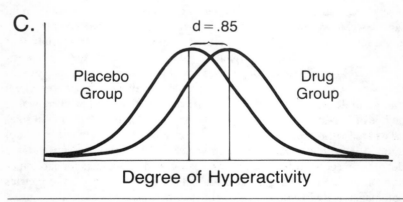

C.

d = .85

Placebo
Group

Drug
Group

Degree of Hyperactivity

Figure 5.2: Three Hypothetical Relations Between Drug and Placebo Groups in Hyperactivity Experiments

tion with t-tests or F-tests based on a comparison of two conditions. The d-index expresses the distance between the two group means in terms of their common standard deviation. For example, if d = .40 it means 4/10 of a standard deviation separate the two means.

The hypothetical research results presented in Figure 5.2 will illustrate the d-index. For the research result that supports the null hypothesis (Figure 5.2A), the d-index equals zero. That is, there is no distance between the drug treatment and placebo group means. The second research result (Figure 5.2B) reveals a d-index of .40, that is, the mean of the drug treatment group lies 4/10 of a standard deviation above the placebo group's mean. In the third example, a d-index of .85 is portrayed. Here the group with the higher mean (drug treatment) has a mean which rests 85/100 of a standard deviation above the lower-meaned (placebo) group's mean.

Calculating the d-index is simple. The formula is as follows:

$$d = \frac{X_{1.} - X_{2.}}{SD} \qquad [5]$$

where

$X_{1.}$ and $X_{2.}$ = the two group means and
SD = the average standard deviation of the two groups.

The formula for the d-index assumes that the two groups have equal (or roughly equal) standard deviations. In instances where the researcher does not wish to make the assumption that the standard deviations of the two groups are equal, the d-index can be calculated by using the standard deviation of one group or the other—typically the control group, if it is available.

The d-index is not only simple to compute but it is also scale-free. That is, the standard deviation adjustment in the denominator of the formula means that studies using different measurement scales can be compared or combined.

In many instances reviewers will find that primary researchers do not report the means and standard deviations of the separate groups the reviewer wishes to compare. For such cases Friedman (1968) has provided a computational formula for the d-index that does not require the reviewer to have specific means and standard deviations. This formula is as follows:

$$d = \frac{2t}{\sqrt{df_{error}}} \qquad [6]$$

where

t = the value of the t-test for the associated comparison and
df_{error} = the degrees of freedom associated with the t-test.

The instances where F-tests with single degrees of freedom in the numerator are reported, the t-value in the above formula can be substituted for by the square root of the F-value ($t = \sqrt{F}$).

The d-index may leave something to be desired in terms of its intuitive appeal. For this reason, Cohen (1977) also presented a measure associated with the d-index called U_3. U_3 tells the percentage of the sample with the lower mean that was exceeded by 50% of the scores in the higher-meaned group. Put more informally, U_3 answers the question "What percentage of the scores in the lower-meaned group was exceeded by the average score in the higher-meaned group?" Values for converting the d-index to U_3 are presented in Cohen's (1977) book. For example, the d-index of .40 presented in Figure 5.2B has an associated U_3 value of 65.5.% This means that 65.5% of the scores in the lower-meaned (placebo) group are exceeded by the average score in the higher-meaned (drug treatment) group. For Figure 5.2C, the d-index of .85 is associated with a U_3 of 80.2. Thus, 80.2% of the scores in the lower-meaned (placebo) group are exceeded by the average score in the higher-meaned (drug treatment) group.

Snedecor and Cochran (1967) and Hedges (1980) have shown that the d-index may slightly overestimate the size of an effect in the entire population. However, the bias is minimal if the degrees of freedom associated with the t-test are more than 20. If a reviewer is calculating d-indexes from primary research based on samples smaller than 20, Hedges's (1980) correction factor should be applied.

The r-Index

A second effect size, the r-index, is simply the Pearson product-moment correlation coefficient. This index is familiar to most social scientists but the formula for the r-index requires variances and covariances so it can rarely be applied to the data typically presented in primary research reports. Luckily, in most instances where r-indexes are applicable, primary researchers do report them. If only the t-test value associated with the r-index is given, the r-index value can be calculated using the following formula:

$$r = \sqrt{\frac{t^2}{t^2 + df_{error}}} \qquad [7]$$

Likewise, when a chi-square statistic associated with a 2 × 2 contingency table is given, the r-index can be estimated as follows:

$$r = \sqrt{\frac{\chi^2}{n.}} \qquad [8]$$

with

χ^2 = the chi-square value associated with the comparison and

n. = the total number of observations in the comparison.

Cohen distinguishes the effect size associated with chi-squares by calling it a w-index but in fact it is identical to an r-index when df = 1.

Finally, one problem which may arise for the research reviewer is that different primary researchers may choose different metrics to study the same phenomena. For instance, in the review of the relation between locus of control beliefs and academic achievement, many primary researchers dichotomized locus of control into "internal" and "external" groups and used a t-test to measure statistical significance. Other researchers left the locus of control scales in their continuous form and correlated them with continuous achievement measures. When this occurs the reviewer must convert one metric into the other so that a single metric can be used in the research review. Luckily, the different effect size metrics are easily converted from one to the other. The r-index can be transformed into a d-index by the following formula:

$$d = \frac{2r}{\sqrt{1 - r^2}} \qquad [9]$$

or the d-index into the r-index by:

$$r = \frac{d}{\sqrt{d^2 + 4}} \qquad [10]$$

Statistical Factors Influencing the Size of Effects

In addition to the "true" impact one variable has on another, there are numerous influences on the magnitude of relations revealed in empirical research. Just a few of the more important statistical factors that may influence an effect size will be mentioned here. This introduction will largely be conceptual; for a detailed, technical discussion of these issues, the reader is advised to consult Glass et al. (1981).

The first statistical factor that will influence the magnitude of relations is the reliability of the measurements involved in the study. The less "pure" a measurement is, the less ability it has to detect relations involving the variable of interest. To estimate the impact that unreliability of measures may have on an effect size estimate in a research review, the reviewer might try to obtain the reliabilities (e.g., internal consistencies) of the various measures. These can then be used to see if effect sizes correlate with the reliability of the measures or to estimate what effect sizes would be if all measures were perfectly reliable (see Hunter, Schmidt, & Jackson, 1982, for details on how to perform this estimation).

A second statistical influence on effect size estimates is the choice of the standard deviation used to estimate the variance around group means. As noted above, most reviewers have no choice but to make the assumption that the two group standard deviations are equal to one another because the effect size must be estimated from an associated significance test, which also makes this assumption. However, in instances where information about standard deviations is available and the group variances appear to be unequal, the reviewer should choose one group's standard deviation to always act as the estimate (e.g., the denominator in the d-index). If a treatment and control group are compared, the control group standard deviation should be used. For the U_3 index, this allows the reviewer to state the impact of the treatment in comparison to the untreated population, e.g., "The average treated person scored higher than X% of the untreated population."

A third statistical influence on effect sizes, noted above, is the small sample bias. In addition to the bias in the effect size estimates the reviewer should also be cautious in interpreting any effect size based on small samples, for instance, when the sample size is less than 10. Especially when samples are small, a single extreme value can create an exceptionally large effect size estimate. In general it is a good practice for reviewers to weight the contribution of individual effect sizes to any overall effect estimate by the number of data points the estimate is based upon.

A fourth statistical influence on effect sizes is the number of factors employed in the research design. If factors other than the variable of interest are included in a research design, for instance, in an analysis of variance or a multiple regression, the reviewer is faced with the choice of employing the reduced standard deviation estimate created by the inclusion of the extra factors or attempting to retrieve the standard deviation that would have occurred had all the extraneous factors been ignored (i.e., included in the error estimate). Whenever possible, the latter strategy should be employed by the reviewer; that is, an attempt should be made to calculate the effect size as though the comparison of interest was the sole comparison in the analysis. Practically speaking, however, it is often difficult for a reviewer to retrieve this overall standard deviation estimate. In such cases, the reviewer should examine whether or not the number of factors involved in the experiment is associated with the size of the experimental effect.

The illustrative reviews. Both effect sizes presented above appeared in the illustrative reviews. The r-index was used to measure effect size in the review of the relation between locus of control beliefs and academic achievement. Of the 98 studies, 67 reported enough information to allow an r-index of their results to be computed. The average r-index equalled +.18 (SD = .16) indicating more internal locus of control beliefs were associated with higher academic achievement.

The review of drug treatments of hyperactivity revealed three separate general results. For comparisons between drug treatments and no placebo controls, the mean d-index equalled +1.21. A d-index of this magnitude indicates that the average child in the control group was more hyperactive than 88.5% of the children receiving drug treatment. The d-index for comparisons of drug treatments versus placebo controls d = .84 or U_3 = 79.9%. For the placebo versus no placebo control comparisons, the d-index was .32 and U_3 was 62.5%.

Finally, the effect sizes uncovered in the review of research design effects on response rates to questionnaires were expressed using the r-index (or w-index according to Cohen's terminology). In this case, however, the effect size was not computed by averaging the effects found in separate studies. Instead, because raw data could be retrieved, the overall effect size was based on the cumulation of raw data. For instance, the analysis of the presence versus absence of a monetary incentive on returning the questionnaire found incentives to be superior with r = +.15.

ANALYZING VARIANCE IN EFFECT
SIZES ACROSS STUDIES

The analytic procedures described thus far have illustrated how to combine the probabilistic results of separate studies and how to generate an estimate of the strength of relations. Another set of statistical techniques help discover why effect sizes vary from one study to another. In these analyses the effect sizes found in the separate studies are the dependent

TABLE 5.2
A Hypothetical Example of the Analysis of Eight Comparisons

Study	n	t	d	f	w	λ	r
1	24	1.99	+.59	12	11.51	−1	.28
2	14	0	0	7	7.00	−1	0
3	16	.46	+.17	8	7.97	−1	.08
4	12	−1.30	−.55	6	5.78	−1	−.27
5	32	2.38	+.60	16	15.29	+1	.29
6	20	.29	+.09	10	10.00	+1	.04
7	10	0	0	5	5.00	+1	0
8	15	1.06	+.40	7.5	7.35	+1	.20

$$\sum_{i=1}^{N} w_i d_i = 11.51(.59) + 7.00(0) + 7.97(.17) \ldots + 7.35(.40) = 17.98$$

$$\sum_{i=1}^{N} w_i = 11.51 + 7.00 + 7.97 + \ldots + 7.35 = 69.90$$

$$d. = 17.98 / 69.90 = .257$$

$$\chi^2 = 11.51(.59 - .257)^2 + 7.00(0 - .257)^2 + \ldots 7.35(.40 - .257)^2 = 8.12$$

$$\chi^2 = 12.74 - \frac{17.98^2}{69.90} = 8.12$$

$$Z_\lambda = -1(.59) + -1(0) \ldots + 1(.40) / \sqrt{\frac{-1^2}{11.51} + \frac{-1^2}{7.00} \ldots + \frac{+1^2}{7.35}} = .88/1.01 = .87$$

variables and the varying characteristics of the studies are the predictor variables. Thus the reviewer asks whether the magnitude of relation between two variables in a study is affected by the way the study was designed or carried out.

Table 5.2 presents some additional facts about the eight hypothetical comparisons originally presented in Table 5.1. The fourth column of Table 5.2 presents the d-index associated with the eight comparisons. The first thing to note is that the size of the eight d-indexes vary from comparison to comparison. An explanation for this variability is not only important but it also represents the most unique contribution of the research review. By performing an analysis of differences in effect sizes the reviewer can gain insight into the factors that affect relationship strengths even though these factors may have never been studied in a single experiment. Assume, for instance, that the first four studies listed in Table 5.2 used only males as participants while the second four studies used only females. Is the strength of relation between the two variables different for males and females? This question could be tentatively answered through the use of the analytic techniques described below, even though no single study employed both males and females.

The techniques that follow are again only a few examples from many procedures for analyzing variance in effects. Their description is conceptual and brief. Those interested in applying the formulas are advised first to examine more detailed treatments (especially Rosenthal, 1984).

Traditional Inference Statistics

The first means for analyzing the variance in effect sizes involves the application of the traditional inference procedures that are employed by primary researchers. Thus if a reviewer of drug treatments of hyperactivity wished to discover whether studies using boys revealed stronger or weaker effects than studies using girls the reviewer might do a t-test on the difference between effect sizes found in studies using exclusively boys versus studies using exclusively girls. Or if the reviewer was interested in whether the effect size was influenced by the length of delay between treatment and the measurement of hyperactivity, the reviewer might correlate the length of delay in each study with its effect size. In this instance the predictor and dependent variables are continuous, so the significance test associated with the correlation coefficient is the appropriate inferential statistic. For more complex questions a reviewer might categorize effect sizes into multifactored groupings—for instance, according to the gender and age of participants—and perform an analysis of variance or multiple regression on effect sizes. For Table 5.2, if a one-way analysis of variance were conducted comparing the first four d-indexes with the second four d-indexes the result would be nonsignificant ($F(1, 6) = .645$).

Standard inference procedures are the techniques most frequently used by quantitative reviewers for examining variance in effects. Glass et al. (1981) detail how this approach is carried out. However, at least three problems arise with the use of traditional inference procedures in research synthesis. The first involves the reviewer's decisions about whether comparisons are independent of one another. To the extent that effect sizes in a quantitative analysis are not independent of one another, an assumption of traditional inference tests will be violated.

A second problem is that traditional inference procedures do not test the hypothesis that the variability in effect sizes is due solely to sampling error (see the discussion of variability in main effects earlier in this chapter). Therefore the traditional inference procedures can reveal associations between design characteristics and study results without also indicating that the overall variance in effects is no greater than that expected by chance.

Finally, because effect sizes can be based on different numbers of data points (sample sizes), they can have different sampling variances associated with them. If this is the case, the effect sizes violate the assumption of homogeneity of variance that underlies traditional inference tests.

Homogeneity Analyses

A second set of techniques overcome the problems associated with the traditional procedures. Homogeneity statistics ask the question: "Is the variance in effect sizes significantly different from that expected by sampling error?" If the answer is no, then some methodologists suggest the reviewer might end the analysis there. After all, chance or sampling error is the simplest and most parsimonious explanation. If the answer is yes, that is, if the effect sizes display significantly greater variability than expected by chance, the reviewer should then begin to examine other potential sources of variance.

An approach to homogeneity analysis will be described that was introduced simultaneously by Rosenthal and Rubin (1982) and Hedges (1982a). The formula presented by Rosenthal and Rubin will be given here and the procedures using d-indexes will be described first. To perform this analysis, two pieces of information are needed from the primary research reports: the number of participants in each condition and the t-value associated with the comparison (the d-index is also needed but it can be derived from these values). With this information, the reviewer calculates a value called f, which is used to adjust for the number of data points in a comparison. The f for each comparison is calculated as follows:

$$f_i = \frac{n_1 n_2}{(n_1 + n_2)} \qquad [11]$$

where

n_1 and n_2 = the number of data points in group one and group two of the comparison.

The value of f is then used in a formula to calculate the value w, a weighting for the d-indexes. The w-weight is calculated as follows:

$$w_i = \frac{f_i}{1 + \dfrac{t^2}{2(n_1 + n_2 - 2)}} \qquad [12]$$

with all terms defined as above. Next, the w-weighting factors for each comparison are used to calculate a weighted average d-index. The weighted average d-index is calculated as follows:

$$d = \frac{\sum\limits_{i=1}^{N} w_i d_i}{\sum\limits_{i=1}^{N} w_i} \qquad [13]$$

with all terms defined as above.

Finally, the weighted average d-index, the separate d-indexes and the w-weights are used to calculate a chi-square statistic. The formula for this test statistic is as follows:

$$\chi^2_{(N-1)} = \sum_{i=1}^{N} w_i (d_i - d.)^2 \qquad [14]$$

with all terms defined as above.

When the number of comparisons gets large, a somewhat less cumbersome computational formula for this chi-square statistic was given by Hedges (1982a):

$$\chi^2_{(N-1)} = \sum_{i=1}^{N} w_i d_i^2 - \frac{\left(\sum_{i=1}^{N} w_i d_i\right)^2}{\sum_{i=1}^{N} w_i} \qquad [15]$$

with all values defined as above.

The chi-square value can be referred to tabled critical values of chi-square to determine whether the variance in effect sizes is greater than that expected by chance. The degrees of freedom associated with the chi-square value equals $N - 1$ where N is the number of comparisons in the analysis.

Table 5.2 contains an example of how a homogeneity analysis is carried out. For this data set, the chi-square value equalled 8.12, which is not significant with 7 degrees of freedom. Thus it would be concluded that the amount of variability demonstrated in this set of d-indexes was not significantly greater than that expected by chance.

Rosenthal and Rubin (1982) and Hedges (1982b) also present a formula for carrying out planned contrasts between groupings of effect sizes. Planned contrasts can be carried out if the homogeneity statistics were not significant, or if the reviewer has a strong rationale for doing so. In the sixth column in Table 5.2 a set of Lambda (λ) weights are presented that could be used to determine whether the effect sizes observed in the first four studies differ significantly from those observed in the second four studies. In all instances, the sum of the λ weights in a contrast should equal zero (see any standard analysis of variance textbook for the basic ground rules on how independent contrasts are performed). The formula for generating a Z-score that tests for the significance of the planned contrast is:

$$Z_\lambda = \frac{\sum_{i=1}^{N} \lambda_i d_i}{\sqrt{\sum_{i=1}^{N} \frac{\lambda_i^2}{w_i}}} \qquad [16]$$

with all terms defined as above.

Table 5.2 contains an example of a planned contrast between the first four and second four d-indexes. This contrast Z-score equals .87 which is again nonsignificant. Thus, using a contrast procedure, a similar conclusion would be drawn to that associated with the traditional analysis of variance; that is, the two groups of effect sizes do not significantly differ from one another.

The comparable formulas for carrying out a homogeneity analysis on r-indexes are simpler. First, the r-indexes are transformed into their Fisher's Z-equivalents. Next the reviewer calculates the average Fisher's Z-equivalent using the following formula (Rosenthal, 1982a):

$$Z. = \frac{\sum_{i=1}^{N} (n_i - 3) Z_i}{\sum_{i=1}^{N} (n_i - 3)} \qquad [17]$$

where

n_i = the number of observations in the ith Z-equivalent and all other terms are defined as above.

The average Fisher's Z-equivalent is then used in the following chi-square formula:

$$\chi^2_{(N-1)} = \sum_{i=1}^{N} (n_i - 3)(Z_i - Z.)^2 \qquad [18]$$

with all terms defined as above. The resulting chi-square value is again compared to critical values for chi-square associated with N – 1 degrees of freedom, where N equals the number of comparisons.

The most important problem associated with the use of homogeneity statistics involves their practical application. In many instances the reviewer will be confronted with incomplete data reports, particularly when nonsignificant effects are found. It was suggested above that a conservative procedure was to set these effect sizes at zero. However, if the proportion of assumed zero effects is large but an effect actually exists in the population, greater variance in effect sizes may be estimated using this convention than would be the case if complete information on effect sizes were available. Thus while the assumption that researchers reporting null findings without statistics found effect sizes equal to exactly zero will have a conservative impact on combined probabilities and estimates of average effect size, this assumption may lead to larger chi-square homeogeneity statistics if relations actually exist.

A second problem with homogeneity statistics is that they appear to be low in power. If so, important relations may be missed when homogeneity statistics are used along with conventional levels of statistical significance.

A final problem is that the results of homogeneity statistics depend somewhat on the choice of the effect size metric. For instance, the same set of data can yield different results depending on whether d-indexes or r-indexes are used to express relations. This is because d-indexes and r-indexes are not related by a linear transform. The problem of nonequivalent results also appears in primary data analysis; that is, the same data analyzed with parametric and nonparametric statistics can yield different results. However, in primary statistical analyses the differences between one technique and another are well established and the relative appropriateness of one technique or another is fairly easy to evaluate. With the homogeneity statistics these ground rules are not yet clear.

In sum, the quantitative analysis of effect sizes is an extremely new field. Problems in interpretation and bugs in the formulas as well as the precise statistical properties of formulas are still being discovered. While it is clear that a formal analysis of effect sizes should be an integral part of any integrative research review containing large numbers of comparisons, it is also clear that at present reviewers must take great care in the application of these statistics and in the description of how they were applied.

Raw Data Analysis

In instances where raw data from comparisons are available, the moderating hypotheses examined by the homogeneity statistics can be tested by the presence or absence of statistical interactions. That is, the reviewer can perform a mixed-model analysis of variance on the accumulated raw data, using comparison characteristics as between-groups factors and the within-study comparisons as the within-groups factor. If the influence of any within-comparison effect is dependent upon the research design, it will appear as a significant interaction in the analysis. A significant main effect attributable to research characteristics (the between-groups factor) would indicate that the overall mean on the dependent variable varied from one group of studies to the other. For example, suppose 12 studies of drug treatment effects on children's hyperactivity were found and the raw data from each was available. In addition assume that 6 of these studies were conducted on boys only and 6 conducted on girls only. The reviewer could conduct an analysis so that drug versus control groups was the within-groups factor and boys versus girls was the between-groups factor. A significant main effect for the drug versus control comparison would indicate study-generated evidence for a drug effect. A significant main effect for gender would indicate that comparisons using one gender revealed greater levels of hyperactivity than comparisons using the other gender. Finally, significant interaction between gender and treatment would indicate that the effect of the drug treatment depended on whether or not the sampled children were boys or girls.

As mentioned above, the practical utility of the raw data analysis is limited both by the infrequency with which raw data can be obtained and by the use of different measurement scales by different researchers.

Variance in Effect Sizes and Review-Generated Evidence

The evidence uncovered through an examination of variance in effect sizes is review-generated evidence, as discussed in Chapter 2. That is, relations between study characteristics and effect sizes cannot be interpreted by the reviewer as uncovering causal relations. In many instances different methodological characteristics of studies will be correlated with one another and it will be impossible to tell which of the correlated characteristics is the true causal agent. Therefore, while review-generated evidence is unique to the research review and represents an important addition to our information and understanding of research topics, statements of causality based on review-generated evidence are very risky. Typically, when review-generated evidence indicates a relation exists, it is used by the reviewer to point out future fruitful directions for primary researchers.

The illustrative reviews. Two of the illustrative reviews, on locus of control beliefs and achievement and on drug treatments of hyperactivity, employed traditional inference procedures for drawing distinctions in effect size magnitudes. In both instances simple one-way analyses of variance and bivariate correlations were employed. Selected results from these analyses will be presented in the next chapter. More sophisticated analyses involving multiple regression and multifactored analyses of variance could also have been carried out. These might have uncovered interactions between design characteristics. However, in both instances the number of design characteristics of interest was so great that more complex analyses would have made the presentation of results very cumbersome.

VALIDITY ISSUES IN RESEARCH SYNTHESIS

The first threat to validity arising during the analysis and interpretation stage is that the rules of inference a reviewer employs may be inappropriate. In nonquantitative reviews the appropriateness of inference rules is difficult to assess because the reviewer rarely makes them explicit. In quantitative reviews the suppositions underlying statistical tests are generally known and some statistical biases in reviews can be removed. A complete testing of inference rules may never be possible but the users of quantitative reviews can decide at least informally whether the statistical assumptions have been met. Regardless of the strategy used, the possibility always exists that the reviewer has used an invalid rule for inferring a characteristic of the target population.

The second threat to validity introduced during analysis and interpretation is that review-generated evidence may be misinterpreted as supporting statements of causality. It has been noted several times in the text that any variable or relation within a review can be examined through either study- or review-generated evidence. However, the scientific status of conclusions based on the different types of evidence can be quite different. Specifically, study-generated evidence is capable of establishing causal precedence among variables while review-generated evidence is always purely associational.

Protecting Validity

Recommendations about what assumptions are appropriate for reviewers to make about their data will depend on the purposes of a review and the peculiarities of a problem area. This is as true of quantitative procedures as of nonquantitative ones. The only sound general advice is that reviewers should open their rules of inference to public inspection.

1. Reviewers should be as explicit as possible about their guiding assumptions when they convey their conclusions and inferences to readers.

2. If there is any evidence bearing on the validity of the interpretation rules, it should be presented. Without this information the reader cannot evaluate the validity of conclusions. Review reports that do not address this issue ought to be considered incomplete.

3. Reviewers should be careful to distinguish study- and review-generated evidence. Even if the number of studies using each design characteristic is large, the possibility exists that some other unknown methodological feature is correlated with the one involved in an uncovered relation. The more equivocal nature of review-generated inferences means that if this type of evidence indicates that a relation exists, the reviewer should call for the relation to be tested within a single study.

EXERCISES

Study	N	Z-score (one-tailed)	d-index
1	366	-0.84	-.08
2	96	1.55	.35
3	280	3.29	.47
4	122	0	.00
5	154	1.96	.33
6	120	2.05	.41
7	144	-1.64	-.28

1. What is the combined Z-score and probability level of the seven studies listed above using the Adding Zs method? Using the Adding Weighted Zs method? What is the Fail-safe N?

2. What is the average unweighted d-index? What is the average d-index weighted by sample size?

3. Are the effect sizes of the seven studies homogeneous?

6

The Public
Presentation Stage

It is proposed that reviews employ a reporting format similar to primary research reports, including introduction, methods, results, and discussion sections. Special attention is given to discussing how tabulated data can be used in reviews and how effect sizes can be substantively interpreted. Finally, the chapter describes threats to validity that arise from poor reporting and how to protect against them.

Research is complete only when the results are shared with the scientific community (APA, 1983, p. 17).

The translation of an inquirer's notes, printouts, and remembrances into a public document describing the project is a task with profound implications for the accumulation of knowledge. The importance of the public presentation of results is readily acknowledged but suggestions about how dissemination is best carried out are limited.

REPORT WRITING IN THE
TWO TYPES OF INQUIRY

The codified guidelines for reporting primary research focus mainly on the form of presentation. The American Psychological Association's *Publication Manual* (1983) is quite specific about the style and format of reports. Much less detailed assistance is provided for determining what specific aspects and conclusions of a study the researcher should deem important. For instance, the *Manual* tells researchers to report statistical data and to do so in the results section of the manuscript. However most researchers perform more statistical tests than they think will interest readers. The *Manual* is much less explicit in guiding judgments about what makes a finding important to readers.

Obviously the *Manual* is not to be faulted for this omission. Any guidelines for defining the scientific importance of information would need to be separately explicated for a huge array of different topic areas at specific junctures of problem development (Gallo, 1978). Statistical significance cannot be offered as a general guideline, because a null result may be of great interest in some topic areas.

The research reviewer's dilemma is similar in kind to that of the primary researcher but the dilemma is more dramatic in degree. The reviewer has no formal guidelines similar to the *Publication Manual* which describe how to structure the final report. At best the reviewer follows informal guidelines provided by research reviews on the same or related topics. In most cases the reviewer chooses a format convenient for the particular review problem.

The lack of reporting guidelines for reviewers is a problem because differences in editorial judgments create variance in reviews. This variation is not found in the magnitude or direction of conclusions but in whether particular aspects and results of reviews are included in the report. One reviewer may believe that a methodological characteristic or result of the review would only clutter the manuscript. A second reviewer might think the same piece of information would be of interest to some readers and decide that the "clutter" was worthwhile.

A FORMAT FOR INTEGRATIVE
RESEARCH REVIEW REPORTS

Throughout this book rigorous and systematic rules for conducting primary research have been extended to integrative research reviews. It should not be surprising, then, to find that suggestions concerning the format of integrative review reports draw heavily upon how primary research is presently reported. The basic division of primary research reports into four sections—introduction, methods, results, and discussion—should serve nicely as a structure for integrative reviews. The division of reports into these four sections serves to highlight the types of information that need to be presented in order for readers to evaluate adequately the validity and utility of the review. In the paragraphs that follow, suggestions will be made about some of the information that should be included in integrative research review reports.

The Introduction Section

The introduction to a research review sets the stage for the empirical results that follow. It should contain a conceptual presentation of the research problem and a statement of the problem's significance. In primary research reports, introductions are typically short. Citations are restricted to only a few works closely related to the topic of primary interest. In research reviews introductions should be considerably more exhaustive. Reviewers should attempt to present a complete historical overview of the theoretical and methodological problems associated with the research question. Where do the concepts involved in the research problem come from? Are they grounded in theory, as with the notion of locus of control beliefs, or in practical circumstance, as with the notion of hyperactivity? Are there theoretical debates surrounding the meaning or utility of the concepts? How do the existent theories predict the concepts will be related to one another and are there conflicting predictions associated with different theories?

The introduction to an integrative research review must carefully contextualize the problem under consideration. Especially when the reviewer intends to apply statistics in the research integration, it is crucial that ample attention be paid to the qualitative and historical debates surrounding the research problem. Otherwise the reviewer will be open to the criticism that numbers have been crunched together without ample appreciation for the conceptual and theoretical underpinnings that give empirical data their meaning.

As mentioned in Chapter 2, the introduction to an integrative research review is also where the reviewer should discuss previous reviews of the research topic. This review of reviews points out the importance of the new effort and highlights the empirical controversies that the new review hopes to address and resolve.

In sum, the introduction to a research review should present an exhaustive overview of the theoretical and conceptual issues surrounding the research problem and present a general description of prior reviews and the controversies these reviews have created or left unresolved.

The Methods Section

The methods section of an integrative research review will be considerably different from that found in primary research reports though its purpose is the same: to describe operationally how the inquiry was conducted. Although it is difficult to make general suggestions, most review methods sections will need to address six separate sets of questions.

First, the research reviewer should present the details of the literature search itself, including a description of the sources from which studies were retrieved. In addition, when abstract and indexing services and bibliographies are searched, the reviewer needs to report the years covered in them, the keywords that guided the search, and whether manual or computer searches were used, or both. If personal research is included in the review this should be noted as well. Information on the sources, keywords, and coverage of the literature search is perhaps the most crucial aspect of the methods section. It gives the reader the best indication of the extent of the search and therefore how much credibility to place in the conclusions of the review. The description of the literature search tells the reader how different a personal search of the literature might be. In terms of attempted replication, it is the description of the literature search that would be most closely examined when other scholars attempt to understand why different reviews on the same topic area have come to similar or conflicting conclusions.

The second topic that should be addressed in the methods section is the *criteria for relevance* that were applied to the studies uncovered by the literature search. What characteristics of studies we used to determine whether a particular effort was relevant to the topic of interest? How many relevance decisions were based on a reading of report titles? On abstracts? On full reports? What characteristics of studies lead to exclusion? How many studies were excluded for any given reason? For instance, if a review included only studies that appeared in professional journals, how many potentially relevant but unpublished studies that the reviewer was aware of were excluded?

Of equal importance to a description of excluded studies, is a general, qualitative description of the studies that were deemed relevant. For instance, in the review of the effects of drug treatments on childhood hyperactivity, four criteria were met by every study included in the review: (1) the study investigated the effect of drug treatment on children diagnosed as hyperactive; (2) the study employed group comparisons between a drug treatment and control group, a drug and placebo group and/or a placebo and control group; (3) random assignment was employed as part of the design; and (4) a double blind procedure was used to administer the treatment and record the dependent variable.

When readers examine the relevance criteria section of a review, they will be critically evaluating the reviewer's notions about how concepts and operations fit together. Much theoretical debate surrounding the outcome of a particular review may focus on how these decisions were made. Some readers may find that relevance criteria were too broad—operational definitions of concepts were included that they feel were irrelevant. This contention can be addressed by employing these distinctions in analyzing potential moderators of research results. Other readers may find the operational definitions were too narrow. This may lead them to examine the results of excluded studies to determine if their results would affect the review's outcome. In general, however, the relevance criteria describe how the reviewer chose to leap from concepts to operations. A detailed description of this procedure will be central to constructive theoretical and conceptual debate concerning the review's outcome.

In addition to this general description of the included evidence, the methods section is a good place for reviewers to describe *prototypical methodologies*. This presentation of prototypes is necessary in research reviews that cover too many studies to examine each one individually. The reviewer should choose several studies that exemplify the methods used by many studies and present the specific details of these research efforts. In instances where only a few studies are found to be relevant, this process may not be necessary—the description of the methods used in a study can be combined with the description of the study's results.

A fourth important topic to be covered under methods involves the reviewer's choice of *how independent hypotheses tests were identified*. An explanation of the criteria used to determine whether multiple hypotheses tests from the same report or laboratory were treated as independent or dependent data points should be carefully spelled out.

A fifth subsection of methods should describe the *characteristics of primary research studies* that were retrieved and retained for examination as potential moderators of study outcome. Even if some of these characteristics are not formally tested and are not discussed later in the paper, they should be mentioned. This will alert the reader to characteristics the reviewer might be asked to test at a later date. In other words, the reviewer should fully describe the information about each study that was collected on the coding sheets. In the methods section it is not necessary to describe the frequency with which each retrieved characteristic occurred in the literature; this is best presented in the results section.

A final topic to be addressed in the methods section is the *conventions* the reviewer used to facilitate any quantitative analysis of results. Why was a particular effect size metric chosen? Was an adjustment to effect sizes used to remove bias? How were missing outcomes handled? What form of analyses were chosen to combine results of separate studies and to examine the variability in results across studies? This section should contain a rational for each choice of conventions and an analysis of what the impact of each choice might be upon the outcomes of the research review.

The Results Section

In the results section, the reviewer presents a summary description of the literature and the statistical basis for any cumulative findings. Thus the results section is where the synthesis of independent studies is described—the evidence that substantiates any inferences about the literature as a whole. While the results sections of reviews will vary considerably depending on the nature of the research topic and evidence, a general strategy for presenting results might divide the section into five subsections.

In the first subsection, the reviewer should tell readers the total number of independent relevant hypotheses tests, along with a breakdown of the sources of these hypotheses tests. For instance the number of tests found in published versus unpublished reports is sometimes important as is a description of particular journals which provided large numbers of hypotheses tests. Also certain descriptive statistics about the literature should be reported. These would include the average or modal date and range of report appearance; the average or modal number of participants sampled in each study, as well as the range of sample sizes; the frequency of studies employing important participant characteristics, such as gender, age, or status differences; and the geographic locations for studies, if relevant. These are but a few of the potential descriptive statistics that might appear at the beginning of a results section.

In general, the first subsection should give the reader a broad quantitative overview of the literature that complements the qualitative overviews contained in the methods and introduction sections. In addition, it should give the reader a sense of the representativeness of the people, procedures, and circumstances contained in the studies. As mentioned in Chapter 3, there is reason to believe that research reviews will pertain more directly to a target population of all individuals and circumstances than will the separate research efforts in the area. Whatever the outcome of this analysis, this subsection of results allows the reader to access the representativeness of the sampled people and circumstances and therefore the specificity of the review's conclusions.

The second subsection describing results should present the outcomes of combined probability tests covering the main effect relations that were central to the research review. For instance, in the review of the relation between locus of control and academic achievement this section presented the overall, combined probability for all hypotheses tests of a relation between the two variables. No distinctions were made among studies—the most general question was answered. If more than one research problem is central to the review's topic, then all the general questions should be examined.

A third subsection of results should present the effect size analyses. It should begin with a description of the magnitude of the overall effect size, followed by a description of the results for each variable that was tested as a potential moderator of study outcomes.

Next, the reviewer should return to an analysis of combined probabilities for each significant moderator of study outcomes. For instance, suppose the review found a significant difference in the magnitude of a relation depending upon whether males or females were contained in the sample. In such a case it is good practice for the reviewer to perform a combined probability analysis to discover whether the separate combined probabilities are significant for both the male and female subsamples. When a significant moderator of effect sizes is found, it is possible that the relation is not significantly different from zero in some of the subgroups (even though an overall significant difference was found). This second wave of combined probability tests allows the reviewer to discover which of these possible conclusions is warranted.

Finally, the reviewer should devote a subsection to interaction effects found in single studies, if such an analysis is relevant. For instance, Arkin, Cooper, and Kolditz (1980) were interested in summarizing the research on the self-serving bias, that is, on whether individuals assume greater personal responsibility for successful outcomes than for failures. Arkin and colleagues summarized the tests of interactions contained in the covered studies. They found 59 tests for interaction, of which 14 proved significant.

These 14 significant interactions were described in a table which contained p-levels and d-indexes associated with each interaction effect and a short description of the interacting third variable. In other reviews more detailed descriptions of the interactions might be warranted, along with quantitative syntheses of the interaction effects.

In sum, the results section should contain the reviewer's overall quantitative description of the covered literature and a report of the relations and moderators of relations that proved significant across studies. This lays the groundwork for the substantive discussion that follows.

The Discussion Section

The discussion section of a research review serves the same functions served by discussions in primary research. First, the reviewer should present a summary of the major results of the review. Then, the reviewer should describe the effect sizes found in the review and interpret their substantive meaning. Next, the reviewer should examine the results of the review in relation to the conclusions of past reviews. Particularly important would be a discussion of how the results of the present review differ from past reviews and why this difference may have occurred. The reviewer also needs to examine the results in relation to the theories and theoretical debates presented in the introduction. If not covered by one of the above suggestions, a discussion of the generality of any findings, as well as limiting conditions that restrict the applicability of any relations, should be included. For instance, if a relation was found between locus of control beliefs and academic achievement, does this hold true for all age groups, all ethnic backgrounds, and both genders? Finally, the reviewer should include a discussion of research directions that would be fruitful for future primary research.

In general, then, the discussion section in both primary research and research review is used to make suggestions about the substantive interpretation of relations, the sources and resolution of past controversies, and fruitful directions for future research.

The illustrative reviews. Too much space would be needed to adequately present descriptions of the methods, results, and discussion sections of the illustrative reviews. Also much of the material contained in the reports has appeared scattered throughout the book. Selected results will be presented to demonstrate some of the uses of tabulated material in research reviews.

The results section of the review on locus of control beliefs and achievement was organized exactly as suggested above. That is, the first subsection of results presented a general description of the relevant studies. The next subsection presented the overall findings of the combined probability analysis.

The third subsection reported the effect size analysis. The average r-index across all usable comparisons was r = +.18. Most notably, this section presented a breakdown and analysis of effect sizes according to potential moderators of the relation. The average effect size was computed for each subgroup of six potential moderating variables. Traditional inference statistics (t-tests) were used to determine whether each moderator had an impact upon the size of the relationship.

Table 6.1 presents the results of this effect size analysis. The analyses revealed that several of the moderators affected the studies' outcomes. First, male samples tended to produce larger r-indexes (i.e., stronger relations between internality of beliefs and academic achievement) than female samples ($p < .07$). Second, the analysis of age, or educational status, revealed a nonsignificant but negative correlation indicating that r-indexes were larger in younger samples of students. An examination of this breakdown suggested that a curvilinear, rather than a linear, relation might exist between grade level and the size of effect. A formal test for curvilinearity supported this notion ($p < .005$).

Neither the race nor social class of participants was found to affect the relation between locus of control beliefs and achievement. With regard to the measurement of locus of control, a comparison of r-indexes associated with general measures of locus of control versus measures asking only about academic situations was nonsignificant ($p < .12$) but indicated that specific measures tended to be associated with larger effect sizes. Concerning achievement measures, larger effects tended to be associated with studies employing standardized tests than classroom measures ($p < .08$) but no differences in outcomes were found between studies employing standard achievement measures and studies employing standard intelligence tests.

In the final subsection of the results, combined probabilities were recomputed for subgroupings of studies that tended to be, or were, significantly associated with effect size. For instance, a combined probability for studies involving only males was computed as well as a separate combined probability for studies on females only. This analysis revealed that all subgroups still displayed a significant positive relation between internality of locus of control beliefs and academic achievement except for one—studies conducted on children in the first through third grades revealed a combined probability that did not reach or approach significance.

The results section of the review of differences in achievement motivation was divided into six categories of comparisons: (1) comparisons between different socioeconomic groups using American participants; (2) comparisons between American blacks and American whites; (3) comparisons between American whites and other American ethnic groups; (4) com-

TABLE 6.1
Average Effect Size for Subgroupings of
Study Characteristics

Characteristics	Average Correlations	SD	N^a
Gender			
Males	+.20	.14	27
Females	+.11	.18	18
Age			
College	+.14	.15	32
High school	+.23	.10	8
Junior high	+.35	.22	7
Fourth-sixth	+.24	.15	21
First-third	+.04	.06	4
Race			
Black	+.25	.47	3
White	+.25	.17	8
Socioeconomic status			
Middle class	+.26	.11	9
Lower class	+.35	.34	4
Locus of control measure			
General	+.18	.16	15
Specific	+.30	.22	12
Achievement measures			
Classroom-related	+.16	.15	45
Standardized achievement	+.21	.17	36
Standardized intelligence	+.24	.15	12

SOURCE: Reprinted with permission from Findley, M., and Cooper, H. Locus of control and academic achievement: A literature review. *Journal of Personality and Social Psychology*, 1983, *44*, 419-427. Copyright 1983 by the American Psychological Association. Reprinted by permission of the author.
a. N is the number of studies upon which the average correlation and SD are based.

parisons between non-white Americans; (5) comparisons between Americans and other nationalities; and (6) comparisons between non-American nationalities. For instance, the first category presented was studies of socioeconomic status in America. Table 6.2 presents a brief description of the 13 studies that were found to contain comparisons of the achievement strivings of different social class groups in the United States. The mean year of report appearance of these studies was 1969. A total of 5,158 individuals participated in the studies, which ranged in size from 38 to 1,588.

The 13 studies supported the notion that stronger need for achievement is associated with higher economic status. The combined weighted Z-score (equalling 11.44) occurs less than once in a million times by chance, with an associated Fail-safe N of 613. The d-index (not weighted by sample size) across the 13 studies was d = +.33, indicating that the average participant

TABLE 6.2
Comparisons Among Socioeconomic Groups in the United States

Author	Year	Socioeconomic Index[a]	Need for Achievement Measure	Location	Subpopulation	Gender	Education[b]	Direction	Average d-index
Lefkowitz et al.	1980	education and income	modified TAT	NYC	Anglos and Afros	male	college	3 comp. + 1 comp. − not given	+.18
Fleming	1978	education	TAT	MA	Afros	female	college and noncollege adults		0
Dielman et al.	1973	education	item scale	IL	uncontrolled	both	JHS	positive	+.50
Grunfeld et al.	1973	education and occupation	item scale	NY	Catholics and Protestants	males	HS	1 comp. − 1 comp. =	0
Adkins et al.	1972	ethnic groups and location	item scale	various	10 ethnic groups	both	preschool	positive	+.12[c]
Hall	1972	index of status characteristics	TAT and item scale	CA	Anglo and Mexican	both	college	positive	+.22
Jacobs	1972	occupation	TAT	Midwest	mentally handicapped	male	ES	equal	0
Stein	1971	Duncan Scale	item scale	NY	uncontrolled	both	JHS	positive	+.36
Turner	1970	occupation	TAT	South	uncontrolled	male	JHS	positive	+.98
McDonald	1964	education and occupation	item scale	MI	Anglo	both	HS	positive	+.51
Rosen	1961	Hollingshead	TAT	Northeast	6 ethnic groups	males	ES	positive	+.20[c]
Douvan	1958	occupation	TAT	Midwest	uncontrolled	both	HS	1 comp. + 1 comp. =	+.43
Rosen	1956	Hollingshead	TAT	CN	Anglo	male	HS	positive	+.75[c]

SOURCE: Cooper, H.and Tom, D.Social class and ethnic group differences in achievement motivation. In R.Ames and C. Ames (Eds.), *Research on motivation in education.*
Copyright 1984, Academic Press. Reprinted by permission.
a. All SES indexes are based on father's status.
b. ES = elementary school; JHS = junior high school; HS = high school.
c. Estimated from incomplete data.

in the higher SES group had a stronger need for achievement than 63% of the participants in the lower SES group.

The review of drug treatments of hyperactive children was presented in a very short report but it still followed the guidelines presented above.

The d-indexes from the 61 studies were presented in a figure called a stem-and-leaf display (Tukey, 1977). Figure 6.1 reproduces this display. In a stem-and-leaf display, all of the raw data can be presented in a simple graphic form. The data are first ordered according to magnitude and then the researcher chooses an appropriate number of digits to serve as the stems. The stem-and-leaf display is easier to demonstrate than to describe. For instance, column 1 of Figure 6.1 displays the stems, or leading digits, for each of the d-indexes. Column 2 presents the leaves, or trailing digits, for each of the 16 d-indexes associated with drug versus control comparisons. In this instance, the stems are the first two digits of the d-index (units and tenths) and the leaves are the last digit (hundredths). Thus the smallest d-index uncovered by a drug versus control comparison was .34; the next smallest d-index was .36. A stem-and-leaf display is like a histogram where stems represent intervals and leaves are stacked up to express visually the frequency of intervals. So in the drug versus placebo comparisons (third column), d-indexes most frequently fell between values of .60 and .69, where seven d-indexes can be found. At the bottom of the stem-and-leaf display, information is presented on maximum and minimum values, quartile ranges, and means and standard deviations.

Table 6.3 presents the results of the analyses for the effect of monetary incentives from the review of techniques for increasing response rates to questionnaires. Four cumulative response rates are given. The first rate was called the *experimental* response rate. This was the average response rate for the technique in studies which experimentally manipulated the presence or absence of monetary incentives. The *control* response rate was the average of the control group (no technique) conditions in these experimental studies. The *without control* response rate included response rates from all studies which used monetary incentives but had no control condition. The *absent* response rate was for studies that specifically stated that participants did not receive monetary incentives.

A chi-square test of the frequency of questionnaire responding in studies which experimentally manipulated the presence versus absence of a monetary incentive (i.e., 50.5% for monetary rewards vs. 35.2% for no monetary rewards) was highly significant ($\chi^2(1) = 188.1$, $p < .0001$). This result revealed an r-index equal to .15. Further, both prepaid and promised monetary incentives increased responding over no incentive at all (for prepaid, $\chi^2(1) = 145.8$, $p < .0001$, $r = .16$; for promise, $\chi^2(1) = 7.5$, $p < .01$, $r = .05$). Finally, the amount of the incentive paid appeared to have a strong positive relation-

Stem	Drug vs Control	Drug vs Placebo	Placebo vs Control	Total[a]
2.1	5			5
2.0		8		8
1.9	4			4
1.8				
1.7	0	24		024
1.6		1		1
1.5	5	0688		05688
1.4	8	126	3	12368
1.3	2	02		022
1.2				
1.1	16	8		168
1.0		8	6	68
.9	39	12399	3	12333999
.8	4	05	9	0549
.7	9	5		59
.6		1125779		1125779
.5	09	07	0	00079
.4		2489		2489
.3	46	168	8	146688
.2		478		478
.1		56		56
.0		005	00000	00000005
Maximum	2.77	2.08	1.43	2.77
Q_3	1.55	1.30	.93	1.30
Median	1.10	.69	.19	.80
Q_1	.59	.42	.00	.38
Minimum	.34	.00	−1.30	−1.30
Mean	1.21	.84	.32	.84
SD	.67	.54	.72	.60

SOURCE: Ottenbacher, K. and Cooper, H. Drug treatments of hyperactive children. *Developmental Medicine and Child Neurology*, 1983, *25*, 353-357. Copyright 1983 by Spastics International Medical Publications. Reprinted by permission.
a. Two values, 2.77 and −1.30, are not included in the table.

Figure 6.1: d-Indexes for Three Types of Comparisons

ship to response rates. When the amount offered was correlated with the weighted average response rate, the resulting r-index equalled +.61. It was pointed out, of course, that researchers should consider the cost/benefit ratio associated with paying extremely large sums of money for responses.

THE SUBSTANTIVE INTERPRETATION
OF EFFECT SIZE

In quantitative reviews, one function of a discussion section is the interpretation of the size of the relations. Once reviewers have generated an

TABLE 6.3
Effect of Monetary Incentives on Response Rate

Monetary Incentive	Weighted Average Response Rate	Number of Contacts	Number of Response Rates	SD of Response Rates
Experimental	50.5	5,444	49	20.9
Control	35.2	3,133	30	20.2
W/o control	52.2	2,382	15	18.6
Absent	20.1	961	3	21.8
Amount (in dollars)				
0.10	41.6	1,484	17	9.5
0.25	53.9	2,399	10	25.1
0.50	34.7	1,035	9	12.9
1.00	35.9	697	5	19.9
2.00	41.0	200	1	0.0
3.00	40.5	200	1	0.0
5.00	62.1	1,012	13	14.6
10.00	82.0	314	2	5.9
25.00	54.1	205	2	22.5
50.00	75.0	83	1	0.0
Prepaid				
Experimental	42.4	3,551	33	18.0
Control	26.8	2,271	22	14.6
W/o control	54.8	1,614	4	29.0
Promised				
Experimental	58.6	1,696	13	22.2
Control	52.8	796	7	21.9
W/o control	46.8	768	11	15.1

SOURCE: Yu, J. and Cooper, H. A quantitative review of research design effects on response rates to questionnaires. *Journal of Marketing Research*, 1983, *20*, 36-44. Copyright 1983 by the American Marketing Association. Reprinted by permission.

effect size, how are they to know if it is large or small, meaningful or trivial? Since statistical significance cannot be used as a benchmark—i.e., small effects can be statistically significant and large effects nonsignificant—a set of rules must be established for determining the explanatory or practical value of a given effect magnitude.

Cohen (1977) attempted to address the issue of interpreting effect size estimates. He suggested some general definitions for small, medium, and large effect sizes in the social sciences. However, Cohen chose these quantities to reflect the typical effect sizes encountered in the behavioral sciences as a whole—he warned against using his labels to interpret relationship magnitudes within particular social science disciplines or topic areas. His general labels, however, illustrate how to go about interpreting effects and for this purpose they will be reviewed here.

Cohen labelled an effect size small if d = .20 or r = .10. He wrote, "Many effects sought in personality, social, and clinical-psychological research are likely to be small . . . because of the attenuation in validity of the measures employed and the subtlety of the issue frequently involved" (p 13). Large effects, according to Cohen, are frequently "at issue in such fields as sociology, economics, and experimental and physiological psychology, fields characterized by the study of potent variables or the presence of good experimental control or both" (p. 13). Large magnitudes of effect were $d = .80$ or $r = .50$. Medium sized effects were placed between these two extremes, that is $d = .50$ or $r = .30$.

Cohen's reasoning can be used to demonstrate the relative nature of effect sizes. Suppose the review of locus of control and academic achievement revealed an average r-index of $+.30$. How should the relation's magnitude be interpreted? Clearly the interpretation depends on the other relations chosen as contrasting elements. According to Cohen, this is a medium-sized behavioral science effect. Thus, compared to other relations in the behavioral sciences in general, this would be an average effect size, not surprisingly large or small. However, compared to other personality effects, this effect size may best be described as large, if we accept Cohen's suggestion that personality relations are predominantly smaller than $r = .30$.

Comparing a specific effect to effect sizes found in other disciplines or a discipline in general may be interesting but in most instances it is not very informative. The most informative interpretation occurs when the effect size is compared to other effects involving the same or similar variables. For instance, Kuhlman, Findley, Christensen, and Cooper (1981) attempted to interpret substantively the difference in childhood aggressiveness of boys and girls. In their effect size analysis of gender and aggression, they found a d-index equal to .53. Thus the mean aggression exhibited by boys was more than one-half a standard deviation above the mean aggression exhibited by girls. To interpret this finding, Kuhlman and colleagues compared this effect to other effects involving the gender variable. They found three research reviews on gender differences, involving nonverbal sensitivity, persuasability and locus of control. These reviews encompassed over 250 studies and reported d-indexes ranging from .08 to .66. Against this background Kuhlman and colleagues concluded that the gender difference in childhood aggressiveness was larger than most gender effects. It would have also proved informative if the reviewers had been able to compare their effect size estimate to relations involving other variables associated with childhood aggression. However, because the use of effect sizes in research is still relatively new, no other reviews of aggression research containing effect sizes could be located.

In addition to multiple and related choices of contrasting estimates, two other guides for effect size interpretation may be useful. First, reviewers can assess how much any relation might be valued by consumers of research.

This assessment involves the difficult problem of making practical judgments about significance. An example will illustrate the point. Suppose a study done in 1970 showed that motorists who regularly checked their tire pressure got 22 miles per gallon of gasoline, while motorists who did not check their tires got 20 miles per gallon. In each group, the standard deviation of the mean was 4 miles per gallon. This indicates that the average motorist driving 10,000 miles a year and buying gas at 30¢ a gallon saved 45 gallons of gas and $13.50 annually by checking tire pressure. In terms of the d-index, the pressure checkers and noncheckers were separated by one-half a standard deviation (d = .50), or the average tire checker got better mileage than about 69% of the noncheckers. This effect might have been ignored in 1970. Practically speaking, it might have been considered inconsequential. The same results, however, produced in 1983 with gas costing $1.20 a gallon might elicit a much different reaction. Using 45 gallons less of a scarce resource and saving $54.00 annually would be appreciated by most motorists. Thus the researcher might argue convincingly that the result of the experiment had great practical significance.

If the pressure-checking effect is contrasted with other effects on automobile fuel economy (e.g., tune-ups, observing the speed limit), the comparison might still lead to a conclusion that the effect is small. The researcher, however, can argue that although the effect is of relatively small explanatory value, it may still have great practical significance. This judgment could be justified by arguing that small intervals on the gas usage scale represent large intervals on other, societally valued indicators—for example, the amount of oil that needs to be imported.

A final guide to effect size interpretation that involves research methodology has been alluded to several times in the text. When contrasting effect sizes are chosen, the relative size of effects will reflect not only the explanatory power of the relations but also differences in how data were collected. All else being equal, effect sizes based on studies with strict control over extraneous influences should produce larger effects than less controlled studies (i.e., have smaller deviations around the mean). For example, a tire pressure-checking effect on gas mileage of d = .50 found in lab tests may be less impressive than a similar finding obtained under normal driving conditions. Effect sizes will also be a function of the strength of the manipulation (for example, the degree of tire underinflation in unchecked cars), the sensitivity of the measures (for example, counting the number of fill-ups vs. the number of gallons used), and any restrictions on participant populations (for example, all cars vs. only new cars). These illustrations point out only a few methodological considerations that can influence effect size interpretation.

Finally, it should be kept in mind that effect size estimates reported in research reviews are influenced not only by the methodology of the studies reviewed but also by the methodology of the review itself. As Cooper and Arkin (1981) wrote,

> If an unbiased inference is to be made from the effect size estimate, it is that other literature reviews using similar retrieval procedures should expect to uncover similar ES's. Researchers . . . [and] policymakers . . . need to adjust ES estimates dependent upon whatever sources of bias (with whatever impact) they feel may have been present in the particular literature search (p. 227).

Thus it may not be appropriate to assume that the effect size uncovered in a research review is equal to the effect found in the population. The reviewer must determine if the estimate is potentially inflated by an inability to uncover small effect sizes due to bias in the publication process or the literature search.

In sum, Cohen's (1977) labels give only the broadest interpretive yardstick for effect sizes. The most meaningful interpretation of an effect size comes from comparisons to other magnitudes of relation chosen because of their substantive relevance to the topic under study. Complementing this interpretation should be an assessment of the practical value of any explanation and the role of methodology in shaping the conclusion.

The illustrative reviews. The two best examples of how relationship strengths can be interpreted come from the reviews on locus of control and achievement and on questionnaire responding. The average r-index in the former review equalled + .18, indicating that more internal locus of control beliefs were associated with higher academic achievement. This effect would be considered small according to Cohen's benchmarks for the behavioral sciences in general. However, by employing two of the criteria presented above, a more impressive evaluation of the relation could be obtained. First, several methodological considerations mitigated the size of the effect. With regard to how the research review was conducted, all studies that reported null findings and no other information were included in the effect size estimate as having uncovered a correlation equal to exactly zero. Similarly, significant results that gave no statistical information were excluded. These were probably conservative assumptions, given the disproportionate number of studies that obtained results in a positive direction. With regard to the methods of individual studies, the concept of locus of control is highly abstract and instruments used to measure it vary greatly in reliability. Measures used with children have especially low reliabilities. Therefore the magnitude of relation was mitigated by the unreliability of measurements. Finally, with regard to contrasting elements, both academic achievement and locus of control are undoubtedly multidetermined, so it is unlikely that many personality determinants of academic achievement will prove substantially more strongly related to it than locus of control. Each of these points was made in the review's discussion section.

In the review of questionnaire responding, the relative effects of the dozen research design methods were evaluated in comparison to one another, instead of separately. Thus, the contrasting elements were contained in the review itself. For instance, the r-index of $+.16$ associated with prepaid monetary incentives was compared with the r-index of $+.05$ for promised monetary incentives. This was done so that future questionnaire administerers could determine which design characteristics would produce the greatest increase in responding relative to the cost involved in employing that procedure.

VALIDITY ISSUES IN REPORT WRITING

The two threats to validity accompanying report writing relate to the different target populations of the review. First, the omission of details about how the review was conducted is a potential threat to validity. As with primary research, an incomplete report reduces the replicability of the review conclusion. Jackson (1980) examined 36 reviews and found "complete" to be a far-from-accurate description of most reviews:

> Only one of the 36 articles reported the indexes and information retrieval systems used to search for primary studies on the topic. Only three of the 36 reported the bibliographies used as a means of locating studies. Only seven indicated whether or not they analyzed the full set of located studies on the topic, instead of some subset. Only one-half of the 36 reported the direction and magnitude of the findings of any of the reviewed primary studies, and few did this for each finding. In addition, very few review articles systematically reported characteristics of the primary research that may have affected the findings (pp. 456-457).

Without these details, the reader cannot ascertain whether a personal review of the literature would lead to similar findings.

The second validity threat in report writing involves the omission of evidence about moderators of relations that other inquirers may find important. Matheson, Bruce, and Beauchamp (1978) observed that "as research on a specific behavior progresses, more details concerning the experimental conditions are found to be relevant" (p. 265). Thus a review will lose its timeliness if the reviewer is not astute enough to identify the variables and moderators that are (or will be) important to an area. More complete reviews will take longer to be replaced by newer reviews, and will therefore have greater temporal generality.

Protecting validity. Recommendations about how reviewers can protect against these threats to validity are as difficult to offer as recommendations for how primary researchers should approach this stage of inquiry. This chapter is filled with suggestions which might provide a starting point. However, reviewers will never be able to predict perfectly which omitted characteristic or result of their reviews will eventually render their conclusions invalid or obsolete. On the positive side, reviewers certainly want their documents to have long lives. We can anticipate that reviewers give considerable thought to how to present the most exhaustive report in the most readable manner.

EXERCISES

1. Read two integrative research reviews. Outline what the authors tell about each of the following: (a) how the literature search was conducted; (b) what rules were used to decide if studies were relevant to the hypothesis; and (c) what rules were used to decide if cumulative relations existed.

2. Find two primary research reports on the same topic that vary in method. Calculate the effect size reported in each. Compare the effect sizes to one another, taking into account the influence of the different methods. Using other criteria, decide whether you consider each effect size large, medium, or small. Justify your decision.

7

Conclusion

This chapter presents general issues pertaining to how the notion of rigorous research reviewing is likely to evolve in the future as well as some considerations surrounding the feasibility of conducting reviews that meet rigorous criteria. Several issues concerning research reviewing and the philosophy of science are also discussed.

There are several issues related to research reviewing that cannot be placed easily into the packaging of events represented by the five-stage model. These overarching considerations deal with problems and promises in applying the guidelines set forth in the previous chapters.

VALIDITY ISSUES REVISITED

First, the five stages of reviewing contained eleven threats to validity. It is likely that other threats exist that have been overlooked in this treatment. Campbell and Stanley's (1963) list of validity threats to primary research was expanded by Campbell (1969), Bracht and Glass (1968), and Cook and Campbell (1979). This same expansion and re-specification of threats to validity is also likely to occur in the area of research reviewing. It shows progress in the systematization of issues surrounding legitimate scientific inference.

Several of the threats to validity arising in the course of research reviewing are simply holdovers that represent pervasive problems in primary research. For instance, during data collection it was asserted that a threat to the validity of a review was that people contained in the covered studies might not be representative of the target population. This suggests that any threat associated with a particular primary research design is applicable to a review if the design represents a substantial portion of the covered research. In the examination of review-generated evidence, research designs should be carefully examined as potential moderators of study results. The creation of these "nomological nets" (Cronbach & Meehl, 1955) can be one of the research review's most valuable contributions. However, if an assortment of research designs is not contained in a review, then threats associated with the dominant designs also threaten the review's conclusions.

FEASIBILITY AND COST

It will be considerably more expensive for inquirers to undertake reviews using the guidelines set forth in this book than to conduct reviews in the traditional manner. Money is needed to conduct computer searches and pay data collectors. Hours are needed to develop evaluative criteria and coding frames and to run analyses. Probably more than one person should be involved, at least in the data evaluation stage.

Should a potential reviewer with limited resources be discouraged from undertaking a project? Certainly not. Just as the perfect, irrefutable primary study has never been conducted, so too the perfect review remains an ideal. As much as the suggestions of this book have been presented as guidelines for conducting reviews, they are also presented as yardsticks for evaluating reviews. In fact, the reader should be aware of several instances in which the illustrative research reviews fell short of complete adherence to the abstract guidelines. A potential reviewer should not hold the guidelines as absolute criteria that must be met but rather as targets that help the reviewer refine the proposed procedures and breadth of a review until a good balance between rigor and feasibility is struck.

THE SCIENTIFIC METHOD AND DISCONFIRMATION

While the pragmatics of conducting research reviews may mean the inquirer must settle for a less-than-perfect product, this does not mean that the ideals of science need not be strictly applied to the research review process. The crucial scientific element that has been missing from traditional reviewing procedures has been the potential for the disconfirmation of the reviewer's prior beliefs. In most instances, primary researchers undertake their work with some recognition that the results of their study may alter their belief system. Not so the traditional reviewer. By extending the scientific method to research reviews, the reviewer accepts the potential for disconfirmation. Ross and Lepper (1980) have stated this position nicely:

> We know all too well that the scientific method is not immune to the diseases of biases assimilation, causal explanation, and a host of other nagging afflictions; scientists can be blind, sometimes deliberately so, to unanticipated or uncongenial interpretations of their data and recalcitrant in their theoretical allegiances. . . . Nevertheless, it is the scientific method . . . that has often been responsible for increasing human understanding of the natural and social world. Despite its flaws, it remains the best means of delivering us from the errors of intuitive beliefs and intuitive methods for testing those beliefs (p. 33).

SCIENTIFIC RESEARCH REVIEWING
AND CREATIVITY

One objection to the introduction of systematic guidelines for research reviews is that such a systematization will stifle creativity. Critics who raise this issue think the rules for conducting and reporting primary research are a "straitjacket" on innovative thinking. I cannot disagree more. Rigorous criteria will not produce reviews that are mechanical and uncreative. The expertise and intuition of the reviewer will be challenged to capitalize on or create opportunities to obtain, evaluate, and analyze information unique to each problem area. I hope the illustrative reviews have demonstrated the diversity and complexity of issues that confront reviewers who adopt the scientific method. These challenges are *created* by scientific rules.

CONCLUSION

This book began with the supposition that research reviewing was a data-gathering exercise which needed to be evaluated against scientific criteria. Because of the growth in empirical research, the increased access to information, and the new techniques for research synthesis, the conclusions of research reviews will become less and less trustworthy unless something is done to systematize the process and make it more rigorous. It is hoped that the concepts presented here have convinced readers that it is feasible and desirable for social scientists to require more rigorous reviews, with greater potential for creating consensus among scholars and for focusing discussion on specific and testable areas of disagreement when conflict does exist. Because of the increasing role that research reviews play in our definition of knowledge, these adjustments in procedures are inevitable if social scientists hope to retain their claim to objectivity.

REFERENCES

American Psychological Association. (1983). *Publication manual* (3rd ed.). Washington, D.C.: Author.

Arkin, R., Cooper, H., & Kolditz, T. (1980). A statistical review of the literature concerning the self-serving attribution bias in interpersonal influence situations. *Journal of Personality, 48*, 435-448.

Bakan, D. (1966). The test of significance in psychological research. *Psychological Bulletin, 66*, 423-437.

Barber, T. (1978). Expecting expectancy effects: Biased data analyses and failure to exclude alternative interpretations in experimenter expectancy research. *The Behavioral and Brain Sciences, 3*, 388-390.

Barnett, V., & Lewis, T. (1978). *Outliers in statistical data*. New York: Wiley.

Bar-Tal, D., & Bar Zohar, Y. (1977). The relationship between perception of locus of control and academic achievement. *Contemporary Educational Psychology, 2*, 181-199.

Bem, D. (1967). Self-perception: An alternative interpretation of cognitive dissonance phenomena. *Psychological Review, 74*, 183-200.

Boyce, B., & Banning, C. (1979). Data accuracy in citation studies. *RQ, 18* (4), 349-350.

Bracht, G., & Glass, G. (1968). The external validity of experiments. *American Educational Research Journal, 5*, 437-474.

Bradley, J. (1981). Pernicious publication practices. *Bulletin of Psychonomic Society, 18*, 31-34.

Campbell, D. (1969). Reforms as experiments. *American Psychologist, 24*, 409-429.

Campbell, D., & Stanley, J. (1963). *Experimental and quasi-experimental designs for research*. Chicago: Rand McNally.

Carlsmith, J., Ellsworth, P., & Aronson, E. (1976). *Methods of research in social psychology*. Reading, MA: Addison-Wesley.

Cicchetti, D., & Eron, L. (1979). The reliability of manuscript reviewing for the *Journal of Abnormal Psychology 1979. Proceedings of the American Statistical Association* (Social Statistics Section), *22*, 596-600.

Cohen, J. (1977). *Statistical power analysis for the behavior sciences* (rev. ed.). New York: Academic Press.

Cook, T., & Campbell, D. (1979). *Quasi-experimentation*. Chicago: Rand McNally.

Cook, T., & Leviton, L. (1981). Reviewing the literature: A comparison of traditional methods with meta-analysis. *Journal of Personality, 48*, 449-471.

Cooper, H. (1983). Methodological determinants of outcomes of synthesis of research literature. In P. Wortman (Chair), *An analysis of methodologies used in synthesizing research on desegregation and student achievement.* Symposium conducted at the annual meeting of the American Educational Research Association, Montreal.

Cooper, H. (1979). Statistically combining independent studies: A meta-analysis of sex differences in conformity research. *Journal of Personality and Social Psychology, 37*, 131-146.

Cooper, H., & Arkin, R. (1981). On quantitative reviewing. *Journal of Personality, 49*, 225-230.

Cooper, H., Burger, J., & Good, T. (1981). Gender differences in the academic locus of control beliefs of young children. *Journal of Personality and Social Psychology, 40,* 562-572.

Cooper, H., & Rosenthal, R. (1980). Statistical versus traditional procedures for summarizing research findings. *Psychological Bulletin, 87,* 442-449.

Cooper, H., & Tom, D. (1984). Social class and ethnic group differences in achievement motivation. In R. Ames, & C. Ames (Eds.), *Research on motivation in education* (Vol. 1). New York: Academic Press.

Cornfield, J., & Tukey, J. (1956). Average values of mean squares in factorials. *The Annals of Mathematic Statistics, 27,* 907-949.

Crandall, V., Katkovsky, W., & Crandall, V. (1965). Children's beliefs in their own control of reinforcement in intellectual-academic achievement situations. *Child Development, 36,* 91-109.

Crane, D. (1969). Social structure in a group of scientists: A test of the "invisible college" hypothesis. *American Sociological Review, 34,* 335-352.

Cronbach, L., & Meehl, P. (1955). Construct validity in psychological tests. *Psychological Bulletin, 52,* 281-302.

Cuadra, C., & Katter, R. (1967). Opening the black box of relevance. *Journal of Documentation, 23,* 291-303.

Davidson, D. (1977). The effects of individual differences of cognitive style on judgements of document relevance. *Journal of the American Society for Information Science, 8,* 273-284.

Edgington, E. (1967). Statistical inference from N=1 experiments. *Journal of Psychology, 65,* 195-199.

Eysenck, H. (1978). An exercise in mega-silliness. *American Psychologist, 33,* 517.

Feinberg, R. (1981). Positive side effects of on-line information retrieval. *Teaching of Psychology, 8,* 51-52.

Festinger, L., & Carlsmith, B. (1959). Cognitive consequences of forced compliance. *Journal of Abnormal and Social Psychology, 58,* 203-210.

Findley, M., & Cooper, H. (1983). Locus of control and academic achievement: A literature review. *Journal of Personality and Social Psychology, 44,* 419-427.

Findley, M., & Cooper, H. (1981). A comparison of introductory social psychology textbook citations in five research areas. *Personality and Social Psychology Bulletin, 7,* 173-176.

Friedman, H. (1968). Magnitude of experimental effect and a table for its rapid estimation. *Psychological Bulletin, 70,* 245-251.

Gage, N. (1978). *The scientific basis of the art of teaching.* New York: Teachers College Press.

Gallo, P. (1978). Meta-analysis—A mixed meta-phor? *American Psychologist, 33,* 515-517.

Garvey, W., & Griffith, B. (1971). Scientific communication: Its role in the conduct of research and creation of knowledge. *American Psychologist, 26,* 349-361.

Glass, G. (1977). Integrating findings: The meta-analysis of research. *Review of research in education Vol. 5.* Itasca, IL: F. E. Peacock.

Glass, G. (1976). Primary, secondary, and meta-analysis of research. *Educational Researcher, 5,* 3-8.

Glass, G., McGaw, B., & Smith, M. (1981). *Meta-analysis in social research.* Beverly Hills: Sage.

Glass, G., & Smith, M. (1978). Reply to Eysenck, *American Psychologist, 33,* 517-518.

Gottfredson, S. (1978). Evaluating psychological research reports. *American Psychologist, 33,* 920-934.

Greenwald, A. (1975). Consequences of prejudices against the null hypothesis. *Psychological Bulletin, 82,* 1-20.

Harper, R., Weins, A., & Matarazzo, J. (1978). *Nonverbal communication: The state of the art.* New York: Wiley.

Hedges, L. (1982a). Estimation of effect size from a series of independent experiments. *Psychological Bulletin, 92,* 490-499.

Hedges, L. (1982b). Fitting categorical models to effect sizes from a series of experiments. *Journal of Educational Statistics, 7* (2), 119-137.

Hedges, L. (1980). Unbiased estimation of effect size. *Evaluation in education: An international review series, 4,* 25-27.

Hedges, L., & Olkin, I. (1980). Vote-counting methods in research synthesis. *Psychological Bulletin, 88,* 359-369.

Hunter, J., & Schmidt, F. (1978). Differential and single group validity of employment tests by race: A critical analysis of three recent studies. *Journal of Applied Psychology, 63,* 1-11.

Hunter, J., Schmidt, F., & Jackson, G. (1982). *Meta-analysis: Cumulating research findings across studies.* Beverly Hills: Sage.

Institute for Scientific Information. (1980). *Social Sciences Citation Index.* Philadelphia, PA: Author.

Jackson, G. (1980). Methods for integrative reviews. *Review of Educational Research, 50,* 438-460.

Kanuk, L., & Berensen, C. (1975). Mail surveys and response rates: A literature review. *Journal of Marketing Research, 12,* 440-453.

Kazdin, A., Durac, J., & Agteros, T. (1979). Meta-meta analysis: A new method for evaluating therapy outcome. *Behavioral Research and Therapy, 17,* 397-399.

Kerlinger, F. (1973). *Foundations of behavioral research* (2nd ed.). New York: Holt, Rinehart, and Winston.

Kuhlman, K., Findley, M., Cristensen, C., & Cooper, H. (1981). *Sex differences in childhood aggression: Some additional information* (Tech. Rep. 252). Columbia, MO: Center for Research in Social Behavior, University of Missouri.

Lane, D., & Dunlap, W. (1978). Estimating effect sizes: Bias resulting from the significance criterion in editorial decisions. *British Journal of Mathematical and Statistical Psychology, 31,* 107-112.

Lefkowitz, J., & Fraser, A. (1980). Assessment of achievement and power motivation of blacks and whites, using a black and white TAT, with black and white administrators. *Journal of Applied Psychology, 65,* 685-696.

Lord, C., Ross, L., & Lepper, M. (1979). Biased assimilation and attitude polarization: The effects of prior theories on subsequently considered evidence. *Journal of Personality and Social Psychology, 37,* 2,098-2,109.

Lykken, D. (1968). Statistical significance in psychological research. *Psychological Bulletin, 70,* 151-159.

Maccoby, E., & Jacklin, C. (1974). *The psychology of sex differences.* Stanford: Stanford University Press.

Mahoney, M. (1977). Publication prejudices: An experimental study of confirmatory bias in the peer review system. *Cognitive Therapy and Research, 1,* 161-175.

Mansfield, R., & Bussey, T. (1977). Meta-analysis of research: A rejoinder to Glass. *Educational Researcher, 6,* 3.

Marsh, H., & Ball, S. (1981). Interjudgmental reliability of reviews for the *Journal of Educational Psychology. Journal of Educational Psychology, 73,* 872-880.

Matheson, D., Bruce, R., & Beauchamp, K. (1978). *Experimental psychology.* New York: Holt, Rinehart & Winston.

McClellend, D., Atkinson, J., Clark, R., & Lowel, E. (1953). *The achievement motive.* New York: Appleton-Century-Crofts.

McNemar, Q. (1946). Opinion-attitude methodology. *Psychological Bulletin, 43*, 289-374.

Menzel, H. (1966). Scientific communication: Five themes from sociology. *American Psychologist, 21*, 999-1,004.

Mosteller, F., & Bush, R. (1954). Selected quantitative techniques. In G. Lindzey (Ed.), *Handbook of social psychology* (Vol. 1): *Theory and method.* Cambridge, MA: Addison-Wesley.

Nunnally, J. (1960). The place of statistics in psychology. *Education and Psychological Measurement, 20*, 641-650.

Ottenbacher, K., & Cooper, H. (1983). Drug treatments of hyperactivity in children. *Developmental Medicine and Child Neurology, 25*, 353-357.

Parker, E., & Paisley, W. (1966). Research for psychologists at the interface of the scientist and his information system. *American Psychologist, 21*, 1061-1071,

Peters, D., & Ceci, S. (1982). Peer-review practices of psychological journals: The fate of published articles, submitted again. *The Behavioral and Brain Sciences, 5*, 187-255.

Pillemer, D., & Light, R. (1980). Benefiting from variation in study outcomes. *New Directions for Methodology of Social and Behavioral Science, 5*, 1-11.

Presby, S. (1978). Overly broad categories obscure important differences between therapies. *American Psychologist, 33*, 514-515.

Price, D. (1966). Collaboration in an invisible college. *American Psychologist, 21*, 1011-1018.

Price, D. (1965). Networks of scientific papers. *Science, 149*, 510-515.

Resnick, A. (1961). Relative effectiveness of document titles and abstracts for determining relevance of documents. *Science, 134*, 1004-1006.

Reynolds, P. (1971). *A primer in theory construction.* Indianapolis: Bobbs-Merrill.

Rosenthal, R. (1984). *Meta-analytic procedures for social research.* Beverly Hills, CA: Sage.

Rosenthal, R. (1982). Valid interpretation of quantitative research results. *New Directions for Methodology of Social and Behavioral Science, 12*, 59-75.

Rosenthal, R. (1980). Summarizing significance levels. *New Directions for methodology of Social and Behavioral Science, 5*, 33-46.

Rosenthal, R. (1979a). The "file drawer problem" and tolerance for null results. *Psychological Bulletin, 86*, 638-641.

Rosenthal, R. (1979b). Replications and their relative utility. *Replications in Social Psychology, 1*, 15-23.

Rosenthal, R. (1978a). How often are our numbers wrong? *American Psychologist, 33*, 1005-1008.

Rosenthal, R. (1978b). Combining results of independent studies. *Psychological Bulletin, 85*, 185-193.

Rosenthal, R. (1976). *Experimenter effects in behavioral research.* New York: Appleton-Century-Crofts.

Rosenthal, R., & Rosnow, R. (1975). *Primer of methods for the behavioral sciences.* New York: Wiley.

Rosenthal, R., & Rubin, D. (1982). Comparing effect sizes of independent studies. *Psychological Bulletin, 92*, 500-504.

Rosenthal, R., & Rubin, D. (1978). Interpersonal expectancy effects: The first 345 studies. *The Behavioral and Brain Sciences, 3*, 377-415.

Ross, L., & Lepper, R. (1980). The perseverance of beliefs: Empirical and normative considerations. *New Directions for Methodology of Social and Behavioral Science, 4*, 17-36.

Rotter, J. (1954). *Social learning and clinical psychology.* Englewood Cliffs, NJ: Prentice-Hall.

Saracevic, T. (1970). The concept of "relevance" in information science: A historical review. In T. Saracevic (Ed.), *Introduction to information science.* New York: Bowker.

Scarr, S., & Weber, B. (1978). The reliability of reviews for the *American Psychologist. American Psychologist, 33*, 935.

Scholarly communication: Report of the national enquiry. (1979). Baltimore: Johns Hopkins University Press.

Selltiz, C., Wrightsman, L., & Cook, S. (1976). *Research methods in social relations* (3rd ed.). New York: Holt, Rinehart & Winston.

Simon, J. (1978). *Basic research methods in social science* (2nd ed.). New York: Random House.

Smith, M. (1980). Publication bias and meta-analysis. *Evaluation in Education: An International Review Series, 4,* 22-24.

Smith, M., & Glass, G. (1977). Meta-analysis of psychotherapy outcome studies. *American Psychologist, 32,* 752-760.

Snedecor, G., & Cochran, W. (1967). *Statistical methods* (6th ed.). Ames, IA: University of Iowa Press.

Stoan, S. (1982). Computer searching: A primer for uninformed scholar. *Academe, 68,* 10-15.

Stock, W., Okun, M., Haring, M., Miller, W., Kinney, C., & Ceurvorst, R. (1982). Rigor and data synthesis: A case study of reliability in meta-analysis. *Educational Researcher, 11*(6), 10-14.

Taveggia, T. (1974). Resolving research controversy through empirical cumulation. *Sociological Methods and Research, 2,* 395-407.

Tukey, J. (1977). *Exploratory data analysis.* Reading, MA: Addison-Wesley.

Viana, M. (1980). Statistical methods for summarizing independent correlational results. *Journal of Educational Statistics, 5,* 83-104.

Webb, E., Campbell, D., Schwartz, R., Sechrest, L., & Grove, J. (1981). *Nonreactive measures in the social sciences.* Boston: Houghton Mifflin.

White, C. (1973). *Sources of information in the social sciences.* Chicago: American Library Association.

Williams, B. (1978). *A sampler on sampling.* New York: Wiley.

Wolins, L. (1962). Responsibility for raw data. *American Psychologist, 17,* 657-658.

Wood, D. (1971). User studies: A review of the literature from 1966 to 1970. *Aslib Proceedings, 23,* 11-23.

Xhignesse, L., & Osgood, C. (1967). Bibliographical citation characteristics of the psychological journal network in 1950 and 1960. *American Psychologist, 22,* 779-791.

Yu, J., & Cooper, H. (1983). A quantitative review of research design affects on response rates to questionnaires. *Journal of Marketing Research, 20,* 36-44.

Zuckerman, M., DePaulo, B., & Rosenthal, R. (1981). Verbal and nonverbal communication of deception. In *Advances in experimental social psychology* (Vol. 14). New York: Academic Press.

AUTHOR INDEX

Leviton, L., 24
Lewis, T., 61
Light, R., 21
Lord, C., 63
Lowel, E., 15
Lykken, D., 80, 96

Maccoby, E., 10, 29
Mahoney, M., 62, 77
Mansfield, R., 81
Marsh, H., 64
Matarazzo, J., 10
Matheson, D., 129
McClelland, D., 15
McGaw, B., 65, 72, 83, 102, 105
McNemar, Q., 38
Meehl, P., 131
Menzel, H., 55
Miller, W., 73
Mosteller, F., 92

Nunnally, J., 42, 80

Okun, M., 73
Olkin, I., 90
Osgood, C., 41
Ottenbacher, K., 16, 124

Paisley, W., 39
Parker, E., 39
Peters, D., 64
Pillemer, D., 21
Presby, S., 35
Price, D., 11, 39

Resnik, A., 26

Reynolds, P., 20
Rosenthal, R., 11, 58, 62, 73, 83, 88, 91, 92, 94, 95, 105, 106, 107, 108
Rosnow, R., 11
Ross, L., 63, 132
Rotter, J., 15
Rubin, D., 58, 83, 106, 107

Saracevic, T., 25
Scarr, S., 63
Schmidt, F., 83, 102
Schwartz, R., 21, 22
Sechrest, L., 21, 22
Selltiz, C., 12, 19, 31
Simon, J., 19
Smith, M., 42, 65, 72, 83, 102, 105
Snedecor, G., 100
Stanley, J., 10, 66, 67, 68, 131
Stock, W., 73
Stoan, S., 55

Taveggia, T., 84
Tom, D., 15, 16, 122
Tukey, J., 80, 123

Vianna, M., 83

Webb, E., 21, 22
Weber, B., 63
Weins, A., 10
White, C., 42, 52
Williams, B., 37, 38
Wolins, L., 73
Wood, D., 40
Wrightsman, L., 12, 19, 31

SUBJECT INDEX

A priori exclusion of studies, 65-66, 70
Abstracting services, 37, 43-55, 116
Achievement motivation, 15-16, 22-23, 26, 32-33, 57, 74, 82, 84-85, 120-123, 124
Ancestry approach, 41, 42

Bibliographies, 42-43

Categorizing research methods, 66-71; methods-description, 68-70; mixed-criteria, 70; threats-to-validity, 66-68
Coding sheets, 19, 30-34, 68, 76
Combining probabilities of independent studies, 14, 79, 88-96, 112, 117, 118, 119, 120, 121; assumptions, 88-89; raw data, 94; significance tests, 91-94; vote counting, 89-91
Comparisons. See Units of analysis
Computerized literature search, 9, 52-55, 56, 57
Conceptual relevance of studies, 25-26, 115-116
Confirmatory bias, 62-63, 77, 81

Definitions of reviews, 11
d-index, 98-100, 101, 106-108, 109, 112, 119, 121, 123, 125, 126, 127
Dissertation Abstracts International, 47, 49, 50, 54, 56

Educational Resources Information Center, 43, 45, 47, 48, 49, 53, 56
Effect size, 14, 32, 79, 81, 96-103, 112, 113, 117, 118, 119, 120, 124-129, 130; comparisons between, 107-108; factors affecting, 102-103; substantive interpretation of, 124-129; variability in, 81, 83, 103-111

Fail-safe N, 92-94, 95, 121

Government documents, 43

Hyperactivity (drug treatment of), 16, 23, 26, 27-28, 57, 70, 72, 82, 85-87, 88, 97, 102, 105, 110, 114, 116, 123-124

Independent hypothesis tests. See Units of analysis
Indexing terms, 44-45, 47, 52-55, 56, 57, 58, 59, 115
Invisible college, 39, 41

Journal networks, 41, 42
Judging methodological quality, 13-14, 62, 63-66, 77, 78; biases in judgments, 13, 14, 16, 77; interjudge reliability, 13, 14, 63-65

Keywords. See Indexing terms

Locus of control and academic achievement, 15, 21, 24-25, 27, 30, 43, 45, 49, 56, 70, 74, 76, 95, 101, 103, 110, 114, 118, 119-121, 126, 128

Main effects and interactions, 27, 32, 83-88, 117-118
Methods for locating studies, 37, 38-44, 55; informal, 38-40, 55; primary, 40-42; secondary, 42-44, 55
Multiple operationism, 21-25, 34

Need for achievement. See Achievement motivation

Past reviews (role of), 12, 29-30, 115, 119
Populations of elements, 13, 14, 37-38, 57-58, 129; accessible, 13, 37-38; target, 13, 14, 16, 37-38
Predispositions, 62-63, 66, 75
Problems in data retrieval, 71-74, 77; coding study results, 73-74, 77; library retrieval, 71; results sections, 71-73, 77
Professional meetings, 39-40
Psychological Abstracts, 43, 44-46, 49, 52-53, 56, 59
Publication bias, 41-42, 55-56, 128

Quantitative synthesis, 14, 72, 74, 76, 79-83, 117-119; criticisms of, 81-82; effects on conclusions, 83

ABOUT THE AUTHOR

Harris Cooper is Associate Professor of Psychology and Research Associate of the Center for Research in Social Behavior at the University of Missouri—Columbia. He has also taught at Colgate University, and has been a Postdoctoral Fellow at Harvard University and a Visiting Scholar at Stanford University. He has published articles on numerous facets of research integration and has coauthored nearly a dozen substantive reviews. At present, he is conducting a study on how research syntheses are carried out by expert reviewers, sponsored by the National Institute of Education. In addition to research reviewing, he does research on teacher expectation effects. Dr. Cooper was the first recipient of the American Educational Research Association's Raymond B. Cattell Early Career Award for Programmatic Research.